Skadi

ᛋᚲᚨᚠᛜᛁ

Mother of Wolves &
Goddess of Winter

LADY WOLF

GREEN MAGIC

GREEN MAGIC
53 Brooks Road
Street
Somerset
BA16 0PP
England

www.greenmagicpublishing.com

Designed and typeset by CARRIGBOY, Wells, UK
www.carrigboy.co.uk

ISBN 978-1-915580-02-3

Page 7 image credit: *The half wolf/half woman* © Mel Scott
melartist64@gmail.com
shopvida.com/collections/melartist64@gmail.com

GREEN MAGIC

Introduction

There is a chill in the air as the morning frost slowly begins to melt with the rising sun. Standing bare footed upon brisk cement with my warm coffee in my hand, the steam rising up and mingling with my breath, I welcome the first few days of winter.

It's the fourth of November. Scorpio New Moon energy building. Samhain just days behind us and Yule a few weeks away. There is a sense of foreboding this morning and an urgency to prepare for the unknown that winter brings. Will the snow fall soon? Do we have enough wood? Have I done all I can to stock up, preserve, dry and bottle the goods grown in the garden? Am I ready?

As I close my eyes and greet the new day, I hear a rustling of paws, panting of breath as my spirit animal wolf pack begins to circle me. I am waking up! There is an excitement and eagerness that comes with each new day. A desire to run and grasp the new opportunities with great vigor.

A howl erupts from my gut and rises up as the morning winds blow through my hair. My spirit animal wolf pack howls along with me. We pause and wait ...... we listen ...... What messages does this new day hold?

From the distance I hear *her* answer. A woman, a goddess, friend, matron, sister, teacher, an energy, essence and leader of the pack that I have come to cherish, love, fear and welcome at this time of year. Her howl is a beckoning call to all the wolves to wake up and seize the day.

In my mind I can see her.

She is incredibly tall, clothed in heavy furs and leathers. Her boots make a loud thud with each step. On her back snowshoes are strapped, on her hip a pouch filled with dried meats. Her hair is woven intricately in braids with bones and beads intermixed. Her face kissed by the Sun with a bit of dirt speckling like freckles. Her muscles so large they push against the fabric of her clothing.

With each step she takes towards me and the wolves, excitement builds. The wolves are hungry for food only she can provide – for she is the wild bringer. She is the force of Nature that we all seek to ignite within. She is courage, boldness and strength. She is one that you call to you when you are lost and starving. She is the one who will give you warmth, inviting you to sit beside her great fire in the winter storms of your life. She is one that will challenge you to stand up when you have been knocked down, to rise when you doubt your capabilities. She is the one that will give you no choice but to halt, to push pause and to freeze – for she is bringer of the first frost.

Oh Giant Frost Mother.
Queen of Winter.
Goddess of Snow.
She is the one we call to when we are in need of her great
blanket of white;
that reminds us to pause, slow down and freeze.
Oh Great Winter Mother.
She is one that calls the wolf within you to howl and awaken.
Oh Great Mother of Wolves.
She is the liberator, the challenger, the one who activates
resistance.
Oh Great Skadi.

Now I am ready! Now I can charge into this new day with passion, conviction and determination.

The wolves run with me.

This book is dedicated to the women who raised me.

To my pack of wild ones!

To my grandmother,
Faeanna Ruth Whitenack Kreitzer.
Thank you for teaching me to ask questions,
to stand up for myself and to play!

To my grandmother,
Juanita Scott.
Thank you for raising my father to be such an incredible man.
I never got to meet you but I'm told that I remind him of you.

To my mother,
Mel Scott.
Thank you for teaching me to see things through the eyes
of an artist, to be creative and be myself!

To my sisters,
Gina, Julie, Jennie, Qhua and *Ami.*
Thank you for showing me what sisterhood within
a wolf pack is.

To my daughter and granddaughter,
Shelby and *Mijah.*
Thank you for showing me the meaning
and power of motherhood, for showing me a mirror
of how to better live my life with meaning.

To all who read this book

Thank you for taking time, investing energy in observing my journey into the wildness of Skadi as more than just a character mentioned briefly in sagas and Eddas. Thank you for allowing me to share my experience with her as a source of energy, a mirror, friend and goddess.

Thank you for gifting me with an opportunity to express my imperfect devotion.

To Skadi

Thank you for being wild, untamed and a Giantess in all aspects.

Thank you for sending me the energy of your wolves, they teach me so much and challenge me on a daily basis to be a bit more than the day before.

Thank you for reminding me to laugh instead of rage.

To push pause, halt, reflect and freeze my reactions.

Thank you for allowing me to challenge myself to love myself and all my flaws by looking at you as a mirror rather than a goddess who possesses unobtainable attributes.

The half wolf/half woman © Mel Scott.

Contents

Introduction   3

Chapter One: Her Story   11

Chapter Two: Wild Attributes   26

Chapter Three: Awakening One's Inner Wolf   35

Chapter Four: Eradicating the Lone Wolf Archetype   46

Chapter Five: Mother of Wolves   59

Chapter Six: "Isa" Rune of Skadi   72

Chapter Seven: Goddess of Snow   85

Chapter Eight: Harnessing the Cold   97

Chapter Nine: Njord and Skadi Sacred Union   108

Chapter Ten: Eyes of the Wolf   119

Chapter Eleven: Wolves in Norse Mythology   131

Chapter Twelve: Ceremonies of Devotion   141

Chapter Thirteen: Invoking Skadi   156

Bonus Chapter: Wolf Pack of Ice Queens   162

CHAPTER ONE

Her Story

SKADI – GIANTESS OF THE JÖTENHEIM & REVENGE SEEKER

In order to really get to know anyone, it is important to become acquainted with the landscape they grew up in. Though her story is brief, Skadi is said to be a Giantess from Jötenheim (yo-tun-hame), meaning "World of Giants". In Norse mythology there are nine worlds, with each world being home to different beings. These nine worlds are often depicted as being held on the end of branches and within the roots that offshoot from the World Tree "Yggdrasil".

Jötenheim is the world in between the realm of gods and the realm of men. Known as a vast, untamed, unknown wilderness that is grim, uninviting and home to the most feared of the Norse Giants – the "Jötuns". Historically, the Giants existed long before the gods and even other worlds came about. It was the Giants who were known to be the originals. It is said that many of the gods we know of in Norse mythology are the descendants of the Giants, even Odin himself. Skadi was one of the Frost Giants. The word Giant has been used interchangeably with the word trolls in some circles.

In myths and legends the Jötuns are described as hideous, fierce and ugly monsters that survive off the flesh of men. They represent chaos and the more destructive forces of Nature. Whether one sees them as frightful or a much larger-in-size depiction of the gods is really up to the individual working with them. It is safe to say that they can be both and as both they possess superhuman strengths. While the male Giants were often described as having green skin and fangs, the Giantesses were said to be of exquisite beauty – the kind of beauty that many of the gods would seek to conquer, marry or enjoy.

Their landscape features deep hidden forests and high mountaintops. Very much the realm of the unknown and a place where one could easily become lost or forgotten, if not swallowed up by the landscape, never to be found again.

Is there really a land of giants? Something in our real world must have inspired the early civilizations to believe in something greater than themselves. If you have ever found yourself standing on top of a mountain looking out at the vast wildness then you know what I am referring to. You know that there is some kind of force – you can feel it as your heartbeat races, tears come to your eyes and you just know that there is a greatness that far surpasses our mere mortal existence.

In Norway there is a national park called Jötunheimen – "Home of the Giants." No, I have not actually been there (at least not in this physical form and body that I have now) but when I looked at images of the place there was a stirring within my soul, an awakening or a remembering. Maybe in a past life I stood on the top of one of those mountains and looked out and knew I was in the Land of Giants.

It makes sense that Skadi (Ska-thee) is of the Jötuns. Her strength and ferocious temper is well known throughout the Eddas and myths of the Norse, but what about her love, compassion, devotion and loyalty? After all, Skadi is the daughter of Thiazi – a Frost Giant shapeshifter and son of Olvaldi. While little is known of Thiazi's attributes, he is widely known as the father of the great Giantess Skadi. One of Skadi's most incredible stories is that of her revenge for her father's untimely death. Her short mention in the old stories is of giant stature. She made an impression! She was elevated to the status of goddess.

In the book *The Way of Fire and Ice – The Living Tradition of Norse Paganism* by Ryan Smith he has this to say about Skadi: "One of the most well-known of the Jötnar. Her great wisdom is in the example of her strong, independent personality and willingness to take direct action to achieve justice. If you seek Skadi's guidance, she will urge you to act while helping you find the strength and best way to achieve justice."

Diana Paxson, who is best known as the one of the most influential experts on Norse Paganism, describes Skadi in her book *Essential Asatru – Walking the Path of Norse Paganism* as "Patroness not only for hunting but also for all sports and is especially dear to independent women and those who do jobs usually associated with men."

When I first encountered Skadi it was through Loki, that mischievous God of Chaos. When I get ready for any kind of ceremony or ritual there is much preparation work that occurs. Time is invested in researching, energy is spent gathering, meditating and then there is the actual creating that must occur. That tangible experience that a priestess offers is so that those attending feel something other than the mundane – they step into the magical. While preparing to welcome chaos as catalyst for change, it was Loki who kept pestering me. It felt like chaos and Loki were one and the same.

While engrossed in embracing Loki as master of being unpredictable, I came across the story of how he was able to soothe the vengeful Skadi and get her to laugh. There was something about the visualization in my head when I pictured this muscular woman fiercely determined to march towards her own death in the name of justice whilst laughing, rolling on the ground and holding her stomach laughing to the point of tears streaming down her face. It was in that moment that I knew I had to get to know this woman. Who was she? Was she actually a goddess as I had become accustomed to the definition? Or was she simply a woman from the past who had her own traumas, woes and could still laugh through her pain? Why would those who wrote the sagas go to all the effort to mention her so briefly if she did not possess a giant heart, a giant wildness? Truly she was a Giantess who mirrors to us our own ability to laugh through pain. It's interesting to me that these two figures who clearly hate each other would also inspire many to seek her out and discover who was this Giantess. What happened to her?

Skadi's myth as told in the Eddas:

It is told that Odin, Loki and Honir set out on an adventure as they were known to do from time to time through the vast mountains when they came upon a herd of oxen. They decided to make camp and kill one of the oxen as they were all very hungry from their journey. They built an incredible fire; the wood was burning hot and should have burned the ox meat to a crisp in just a matter of seconds but no matter how much wood they placed upon the fire the meat would not cook for it had been enchanted.

Frustrated and starving they continued to add wood to the flame and after hours and hours of uncooked meat they heard a voice coming from a tall tree nearby. The voice was coming from Thiazi the Giant who was in his large eagle form proclaiming that he could get the meat to cook (after all, some believed he had been the one responsible for its enchantment) if they would simply share with him a few bites. Desperate and beyond hungry they agreed.

So Thiazi the eagle flew down and the meat began to cook. Thiazi took one great bite and then another of the cooked oxen and due to his size he nearly consumed the entire oxen in just two bites. Outraged, Loki swung his staff at Thiazi getting it tangled in his great feathers. Thiazi flew up with Loki still hanging on to the staff screaming as he was lifted up and away from the fire.

Loki distraught and fearful that his might not survive this unwanted flight started thrashing about and screaming as loudly as he could. Then Thiazi struck a deal. He agreed to free Loki if (and only if) Loki would bring him the goddess Idunn and her magic apples from the world Asgard as a gift.

Loki, who valued his life, did just that. He returned to Asgard and tricked the beautiful Idunn into leaving the safety of Asgard. Loki was ever cunning and wise and had concocted a tale of apples so magical that they would put Idunn's golden apples to shame. Idunn had to see them for herself. So she ventured out into the forest where she was snatched up by Thiazi in his eagle form.

With Idunn missing, the gods of Asgard no longer had access to her magical apples and they began to age, withering and wrinkling with such speed that they would soon perish. When the gods learned that Loki was last seen with Idunn, he was threatened with a very painful and lengthy death if he did not return her.

So Loki borrowed Freya's cloak of falcon feathers and flew to Jötenheim. There he found the goddess Idunn and he turned her into a nut and he was carrying her off in his beak heading back to Asgard when Thiazi caught sight.

As Loki approached Asgard, the guards saw a great eagle flying in pursuit. Knowing it to be the Giant who had plotted Idunn's capture, they built an incredible wall out of fire. Loki flew over the fire with Idunn in nut form just in time. But Thiazi the eagle was not so lucky. His wings caught fire and he plummeted to his death.

When Skadi heard of her father's death and that Loki was behind the trickery, she gathered up her weapons and marched right into the Great Hall of Odin, demanding the death of all who had helped kill her father.

Now Odin, being the wise Allfather, was immediately intrigued by this warrior Giantess who dared to interrupt his feasting. Rather than have bloodshed spoil the feast, he made a wager and offered her something in exchange. Odin offered her one of the gods of her choosing as husband and he promised to make her laugh, for she had been so distraught and filled with sorrow since the death of her

15

father. Odin was also cunning, so his gift of a husband could only come from Skadi's selection being based only on their feet.

Skadi (who had her eye on the golden-haired son of Odin & Freya, Balder) agreed, feeling confident that Balder would have the most beautiful of all the feet. So Odin had all the available bachelor gods line up behind a curtain with only their feet showing. Skadi made her selection and to her disappointment she had chosen the God of the Sea, Njord. But a bargain was a bargain and she agreed to marry Njord.

Now the laugh – that was a different matter. With Loki being at fault and having almost killed the gods due to his wager with Thiazi, Odin left it up to him to get the great Giantess to laugh, which would not be an easy task. Loki grabbed a nearby goat and tied one end of a rope around the goat's horns and the other end he tied around his own testicles. He then proceeded to smack the rump of the goat causing it to jump and tug at the rope which in turn caused Loki to jump and yelp as the rope yanked on his tender jewels. This screeching and the pain being inflicted on Loki caused a deep laugh from Skadi.

Thus she was for the time being calmed and her quest for revenge softened. Skadi and Njord were married and since both lived in different realms, a compromise was made. Skadi would spend nine nights with Njord in his realm of the Sea and Njord would spend nine nights with Skadi in her home at the top of the mountain. After eighteen days it was decided that Skadi could not sleep with the sound of crashing waves and she longed for the warmth of her wolfpack. Njord could not sleep with all the constant howling and the chill of the frozen snow. So they mutually ended the marriage and stayed friends.

If you have ever experienced a harsh, cold and snowy winter then you will know firsthand the work involved. Quite a bit of prep goes into getting ready for the snow to fall. This prep is character-building for sure and not for the faint of heart. It goes to show that Skadi and her home of Jötenheim created her strength of character, hard work and fearless devotion to survival and the survival of those she called family or pack.

In the stories it is said that Skadi lived in the highest of the snow covered mountains, with her only companions being a rather large wolf pack. Reaching the top of any mountain requires physical strength. Skadi not only built a home at the top of a mountain but she had to keep it warm and safe against the elements of freezing winds and heavy snow. Chopping wood is no simple task!

Yet, here was a Giantess not afraid of isolation, physically equipped to survive and determined to make the most of her situation. Again, you can learn a lot about an individual when you take time to understand their landscape. If you have ever hiked in the snow then you know that the scenery you once knew changes – everything looks different with snow.

Just last week I took my son's big dog "Gus" on a hike in the mountains. There was snow on the ground, the Sun was shining and there was no wind; which meant perfect weather for an outdoor adventure. Now I have lived here for over nineteen years, I've explored this area so many times that I've lost count. The snow is disorienting! The landmarks I had been familiar with were either covered or looked so different under the snowfall that a bit of panic set it. In my mind I wandered what would possess someone to live on top of a mountain, alone, in the cold of winter? Then my next thought was: "I hope I can find where I parked the car!"

Instinct, trust, patience and the will to survive are all attributes of Skadi. To be a Giantess not just in physical stature but in all things she tackled is inspirational. I found myself on the mountain that I have explored so many times, telling myself that if Skadi could conquer the mountain then so could I.

As a student of life and daughter of the goddess (she being Nature and the Earth that sustains us), I have come across many books. Some were very historical, some very metaphysical, some very matter-of-fact, as if the author had actually met the goddess they were writing about. In my classes, ceremonies and gatherings I have referred to many of these books. Any time a new goddess is embraced, there is a book, article or blog written about them. But what about Skadi? Where were her books?

If you walk into a bookstore tomorrow and look in the metaphysical section then you will find books on Brigid, The Morrigan, Hecate, Sehkmet – just to name a few – but you won't find a book on Skadi. Even after I met her through Loki and his chaos, it was very difficult for me to find an actual book on her. Maybe even two? She is mentioned in many books and, like her brief saga appearance, she is simply given a few lines to describe her grandeur. It is my belief that the time is now, the world is ready! We have been consumed by chaos for years and now it's time for *"he who is the great Lord of Chaos"* to introduce to us this great Giantess once more so that we may move forward out of chaos and find some solace, peace and strength.

In the midst of the global Covid pandemic, there appeared a book of fiction, *The Witch's Heart*, written by Genevieve Gornichec. This book tells the story of Loki and his wife – the witch Angrboda, another of the Norse women who are deeply underrated and very rarely given devotion. From the first page I was hooked. As an avid book reader (thanks to my mother who took me to the library every week of my youth) I could not put this book down. I was consumed! Trapped really, held captive.

This book brought to life Skadi in a way that in my gut shook me. It was as if this author breathed into this mythical being, this seldom spoken about Giantess who was only mentioned briefly; a soul. Skadi became a woman, a lover, a friend and a sister that I could relate to in so many ways. I could see her in myself and myself in her. There was a power in this book and I am so grateful for the distraction that it provided, however brief (I am a very fast reader), for it gave me a greater desire to really dig deep into the mystery of Skadi.

Working with a deity can be tricky. You hear all sorts of things about contacting a deity and my big question with Skadi was: *is she even a deity?* In the path of exploring Wicca, witchcraft and even paganism there is this motivating factor to find one's matron or patron god or goddess. Why? I do not even know!

My childhood was plagued with the One God, the Almighty, The Father! Growing up in a predominantly Christian community this "God" that everyone spoke of, prayed to and feared was not anyone I wanted to connect with. He sounded scary! He sounded super-angry and not at all approachable. So when I come across a person "new to the craft" (as I call them because I believe the terminology "baby witch" to just be degrading) saying that they haven't found their matron or patron goddess or god, I am sure my face gives away my confusion. Why would anyone want to limit themselves to just one when there are SO many different deities from SO many pantheons that you can look to for inspiration!

But then I remember my childhood. It's hard to break away from Christianity. There is a need to connect with, pray to and call upon a specific "higher power" to assist with this life. I get that! It's just the desire for only one that I struggle with. For years I worked with Brigid while also calling upon numerous other goddesses. When Odin came through, that was shocking, unexpected and frankly unwanted! But I thought: *"what the hell?"* What I am trying to say is that in this life of chaos, when it comes to connecting with any of the gods then it is oftentimes best to be fluid and open minded. Just go with it!

When Loki inspired me to connect with Skadi, there was a reason greater than myself. So if I choose to see her as a goddess then it is my definition of goddess that matters. For some, goddess means just what the dictionary defines: "a female deity" and deity is defined as "a god or goddess." That's pretty open. In my practice, I often refer to the Divine as defined by the individual.

The God of my youth did not possess attributes that would fit the description of divine, but others disagree with me and that is fine. We are all individuals and therefore we should all be allowed to connect with god and goddess deities in our own way, shape and form of devotion. That's all this book really is. It's my form of devotion. Do I believe Skadi is a goddess like the God of my youth? One that I should fear, bow down to and answer to? No! Not at all. But is she worthy of devotion? Yes! Aren't we all?

Skadi, while mentioned in basically just one paragraph in the Prose Eddas, has been receiving praise and attention in the past decade. There are more references being made concerning her and her wild aspects. Just the other day whilst researching, I came across a statue of her that I purchased from *www.dryaddesign.com*. It depicts Skadi wearing a wolf skin as a coat, a quiver of arrows on her back, snowshoes, and she is wearing a snake like a scarf. With the statue came a tag which reads: "The Norse goddess Skadi is associated with bow-hunting, skiing, mountains, wolves, winter and all things wild."

Whilst searching, I also found some pendants made in her honor. There is a common theme, that being winter, hunting and animals. As mentioned earlier, in order to survive, one needs to have the know how. Skadi chose to embrace the cold and unpredictable climate of the mountain top. Choosing to live on a mountain is not a simple decision. With any visit to the wild, one should have basic knowledge, that is – if they want to survive the harsh environment.

Skadi was elevated to the status of a winter goddess due to her ability to ski, use snowshoes and otherwise conquer winter. If you embrace winter sports then you know there has to be some skill and technique involved. What I admire about Skadi is her ability to channel her surroundings as a challenge to not just overcome and conquer but to live amongst rather than against.

Now more than ever we need to start embracing and learning from our surroundings. We need to find the strength and activate our own wildness. I believe Skadi is stirring on her mountain and howling out a war cry to stir something within us. In this world of chaos, where control and fear are the dominating battle tactics, Skadi is wanting our attention. Can you hear her howling? Can you hear that wildness within you wanting to howl back? Are you ready to charge into battle and seek revenge for all that you have allowed to be taken from you (emphasis on "allowed")?

Skadi was not a victim, nor was her father. Yet she was loyal and her need to avenge her father was out of loyalty to her blood, her kin. We are not victims. We are all participants in this chaos of the world right now. We all participate differently, but none of us are victims. Revenge is a powerful word and action. With revenge there is always a sacrifice and always a consequence. Will seeking revenge actually make you feel better or will it put you on the same level?

When it comes to Skadi's revenge, she was initially showing force and that she would take an "eye for an eye." Would that have sufficed her? Maybe temporarily. In my life I have been betrayed, stabbed in the back and turned on by those who were very close to me, those I trusted and those that I was loyal to. In my life I have learned that their betrayal had nothing to do with me. So why fight back? Why waste time and energy in "getting someone back?" Let's face it, those people who betray and hurt really are the ones lacking. Not me. My ultimate revenge is to stop giving them power.

People can only hurt you if you give them consent to do so. Just like betrayal, it's only a betrayal if it is defined by that label. When I think of Skadi and her fierceness skiing down the mountain, bursting open the door of Odin's great hall and seeking justice ready to avenge her father's death – that must have been quite the sight! Scary and intimidating indeed. But Odin was wise and offered her a different option. We too can be wise and look at things from many perspectives. We too have many options. In my life I have discovered the best revenge is to do nothing. When people close the door on me I keep it closed. That's their decision and I have a grand life to live and I am content living it.

Skadi's brief mention has inspired many individuals on very personal levels, in this I am not the minority. Her bravery, cold and distant, unreachable persona has also inspired characters in movies. It is rumored that the White Witch, Jadis, in the *Chronicles of Narnia* books by C.S. Lewis was based on the myth of Skadi. In the movie, Jadis is portrayed by actress Tilda Swinton. She is cold, mean and brought about a hundred-year winter. This White Witch is a sorceress; she holds powerful magic – a power that she is not afraid to use. You can see this in Tilda Swinton's portrayal of the White Witch. In her first scene she is entirely clothed in white. She is wearing a long white dress, cloaked in white fur and even her crown is made of icicles.

To some, Skadi is the dreaded Frost Giantess. There is a natural fear that comes along with winter. Snow and freezing temperatures can equal death to those who are unprepared. If you have ever felt the biting cold of freezing weather you know that there is nothing you crave more than a hot fire and a warm meal. To be the bringer of winter comes with a harsh reality and any goddess who wields the snow can be both welcome and an enemy.

Skadi's association with winter and the harsh cold being her domain has linked her to the *Snow Queen* from Hans Christian Andersen. You may recognize a Disney rendition of this fairytale, that being *Frozen*. Some people believe that the main character Elsa is based on Skadi. Both the *Snow Queen* fable and *Frozen* the movie depict a queen who can conjure snow and ice. Both Skadi and the Snow Queen are depicted as traveling about with skis on their feet. It has also been speculated that the Snow Queen is actually Elsa's mother. There is definitely a connection between both the fable and the movie.

After reading the *Snow Queen* fable I couldn't really see the connection with the Norse rendition of Skadi. However, there is clearly a connection between the *Snow Queen* fable and the White Witch from the *Chronicles of Narnia*. My personal preference is the Disney movies *Frozen I & II* as they reference the Norse tradition with runes, trolls and Frost Giants.

Frozen II pays respectful and accurate homage to the indigenous Sami people and culture which are native to Norway, Sweden, Finland and Northern Russia, where it is said Skadi is from. Disney hired a team of Sami advisors to ensure that their culture and people where depicted correctly. The Arctic Sami people (also referred to as Finnar and Laplanders) were part of the Viking culture. These indigenous people were honored and respected in Viking history as skilled sorcerers and shaman practitioners of shapeshifting, possessing power over the animals.

Both the Vikings and Sami people interacted with each other through trades, forming of alliances, marriage unions and mutual respect. There was a blending of cultures which would have allowed myths and legends to intermix.

Hans Christian Andersen grew up in Denmark, so he naturally would have been exposed to Danish folktales that where influenced by the Norse myths and the Sami people. This influence you can clearly see when two ravens are mentioned as being Gerda's guide in the *Snow Queen* fable along with mention of a wild hunt. Both ravens and the wild hunt are deeply connected to Odin, who is Allfather of the Norse. This practice of communicating and working with animals as equals is anchored into animism and the belief that all aspects of nature are divine, whole and sentient beings. This is something that shamans and indigenous people are well known and revered for.

Skadi is one of vast mystery and (as with all deities) she is subject to the individual's connection and relationship with her. What I have found is that you can have a room full of people, mention the name of one goddess and see her described differently by each individual. This book is not meant to be an exact for-the-fact description of Skadi, for no one knows if she was an actual person, goddess or simply a part of the Norse pantheon stories. I am no expert nor do I claim to be. This book is a quest and an offering from one devotee of Skadi to those who can relate to her or are curious to discover insights and other opinions on her. She, like every deity out there, is multifaceted. There are attributes you can relate to, admire, fear or be repelled by, but the connection is yours to determine.

One thing is certain, Skadi is an inspiration. She is a force! There is a sense of foreboding, fear, apprehension, excitement and intrigue that comes with getting to know any deity. On a personal level, I believe that Skadi is surfacing in many facets with a vengeance and she is bringing a message that will create a howl within any individual who sees her, connects with her and honors all that this fierce, frigid, vengeful, wintry, cold-as-ice queen of sovereignty has to offer. She is making her presence known and her wolves are running with her.

MEDITATION ACTIVATION WITH SKADI

Beginning with breath, take a nice slow, conscious inhale and cleansing exhale. Breathe in to the count of four and exhaling out to the count of four (**repeat 4 times**). Allow your body to create its own wave of breath. Trusting that your body will relax and let go with each exhale and that with each inhale your body will activate and heal.

In your mind's eye, picture yourself standing in a forest. It is dark and the ground is covered with snow. There is a quietness that surrounds you in the forest, almost as if the entire forest is at rest. The trees stand tall and vigilant. The ground tucked in under a very thick blanket of white. The stars are clear in the sky above and with each breath you can physically see your exhale leaving your body.

Here in the winter of forest darkness you feel a peaceful calm, yet you also feel a cold creeping in. Far off in the distance, you hear the sound of wolves howling. As you look toward the direction of the howling, you see smoke billowing up in the air. Someone has lit a fire. Seeking warmth, you go towards the source of the smoke, walking upon the snow with your snowshoes, making sure that you do not sink into the cold below.

When you come to the source of the smoke, you see a cabin with wolves lounging about on the front porch. The door is open and you can see light inside. Two of the wolves run up to meet you; at first you stand still honoring their right to defend themselves and their pack. You let them sniff your feet and your legs. Then they began to lead you to the open cabin door.

As you remove your snowshoes to enter, you see inside a very warm fire going, you smell a warm stew brewing in the cast iron cauldron hanging over the fire and you see a very large women dressed in warm fur stoking the fire. She nods your way and motions for you to sit upon a stool that faces the hot fire.

You accept her hospitality, closing the door behind you. When you sit upon the stool, you allow your body to become warm from the fire. The great giant of a woman hands you a cup of stew and a spoon. Together you both sit, watching the fire and eating the stew. Content. Warm. Silent. Warmed inside and out, you start to speak when you are silenced by one stern look. In response, the woman simply offers you one sentence: "There is a time for talking and a time for being silent. Now is the time to sit, be still and just be." That is exactly what you do. You sit and just be (allow yourself time to just sit in silence, no talking, just breathing).

CHAPTER TWO

Wild Attributes

"**H**er Story" in Chapter One shows us that Skadi possessed great physical strength and tenacity. She was possessed with a fierce need for revenge. But are those her main attributes? Is that it? Is she just another angry daughter who wants to kill the person who brought her father to his end? What is it about this Giantess that triggers devotion and appreciation? What is it about this Giantess that sparks curiosity and intrigue?

Any time a new deity comes knocking, visits my dreams or stirs an awakening; there are steps I take – the first being research. After researching comes observation. I am a big list-maker. When I observe something, I list what it is that first engages me, what repulses me and what I will do with this newly obtained information. With Skadi, after reading her short encounter with the gods in Odin's great hall, naturally I sat down and created a list. What was it that made me stop and re-read that story? Was it the actions that took place or one of the characters? Well, Skadi stood out to me, so I made a list of the characteristics that I saw within her.

Confidence is one of the most attractive qualities that one can possess, at least in my opinion. But how does one gain confidence? In order to really embrace confidence, one should understand the basic definition. Confidence is "the feeling or belief that one can rely on someone or something, firm trust, the state of feeling certain about the truth of something." In the case of Skadi, she had complete confidence in her skills and such love of her father that she marched into the great hall and threatened the Allfather! That's some incredible confidence!

Building confidence has to start with accomplishing things. This takes time, energy and effort. It also takes great will power. In order to become confident, one must first feel defeat and get back up. Let's face it, life is not easy. Some days are better than others. The ability to keep going after a setback is a big step in building confidence. Highlighting the journey and progress is another way of staying motivated.

Think of doing strength building. For example, push-ups; when I was testing for the position of officer, one of the physical requirements was to be able to do 25 "man" push-ups consecutively. Well I had never even done one! So I set my goal and started with one, then two, then doubled that. It took some time but with time and perseverance I was able to do the full 25. My confidence level grew because of my stubbornness to not quit. This can be applied to all aspects of life. It takes time, energy and mental will-power.

What I cherish about Skadi is her self confidence. The ability to stand up for those you love and things you believe in mirrors confidence and gives permission for others to do the same. Think of a time when you stood up for yourself and how good you felt afterwards.

Physical strength not only creates confidence but it allows one to feel strong enough to conquer tasks that one may face. For Skadi, she was said to be incredibly strong, large-muscled and let's not forget she was a Giantess. As Goddess of Snowshoeing, she had to possess a level of physical strength that would allow her to trek through the mountains in very extreme weather.

While snowshoeing is rumored to not be difficult to learn, it does require a bit more physical energy than just going on a hike in the mountains in the summertime, with studies showing that the difference between hiking and snowshoeing can be as high as 50% more energy. It can take up to twice the time to cover the same distance in the worst snow conditions and quickly wear out even the most fit hiker. Skadi was not only connected with snowshoeing but all winter sports, such as sledding and skiing, which all require physical endurance, technique and strength.

If you have ever trained for a marathon or sporting event then you know the time, energy and persistence involved. Not to mention the mental strategy necessary to overcome the challenge of doubts and insecurities. Improving one's physical strength has numerous benefits from increased muscle mass, higher calorific burn, stronger joints and bones to increased endurance and inner as well as outer confidence.

Tenacity by definition is the quality or fact of being able to grasp something firmly, the quality of being determined and willing to continue – to persevere and persist despite the odds. Skadi faced odds in numbers when she demanded justice to avenge her father's death. There was only one of her and many in the great hall. Still she continued in her pursuit. She showed great tenacity.

When was the last time you were tenacious? Have you ever suffered a physical injury and kept going? About three years ago I set a goal to do yoga every day. Back in January, while hiking with my sons, I rolled my ankle to the point that we all heard a very loud snap and pop. Despite being in incredible pain and knowing there was something broken, I refused to give up my yoga practice.

There are ways to develop a more tenacious way of life. Set some goals, be specific! I have found that letting others know your goals can be of great help. They will remind you, cheer you on and by doing so they are encouraging you with their tenacious belief in your abilities. Staring fear down is another way of living more tenaciously. This can be a more difficult undertaking but fears are typically self-created, so they can be conquered. I have found that creating a vision board is another way of putting my intentions and goals out into the Universe. While I doubt that Skadi was cutting up magazines and using mod podge to create a revenge vision board, I am sure she did do some serious physical training and mental affirmations as she was marching to demand justice.

Loyalty is one characteristic that in my personal life holds the most meaning. Knowing who is in my circle, who will stand beside me and who I can count on offers me stability. At the same time, reciprocating loyalty is huge! Where I live, we operate on wolf pack modality. Living by the motto of Rudyard Kipling: "The strength of the pack is the wolf and the strength of the wolf is the pack." This just doesn't work if there is disloyalty in the pack or community. Each member has to honor the pack as an individual and work together for the whole or else things crumble.

Skadi was loyal to her father, her family of Giants. She had a job to do and as daughter that was to avenge her father's death. It is my belief that Skadi knew that if she failed that the other Giants would finish what she started.

Skadi also honors the wolf pack modality as she is surrounded by wolves. She is part of the pack and to some she is Mother of Wolves. As one who honors wolf as my primary spirit animal, I have found wolf to be the greatest of all animals, for wolf is one who mirrors physical strength, tenacity, loyalty, compassion, conviction and determination – all attributes that Skadi possesses.

To honor wolf as teacher is to see oneself as part of a pack – to know that you are not alone and that you are vital and you must put in your dues. Wolves are not solitary creatures; their survival relies upon their pack. Loyalty ensures that the pack thrives.

Compassion by definition is sympathetic pity and concern for the sufferings or misfortunes of others. Skadi and Njord both displayed great compassion for each other. Despite being loyal and honoring the vows of marriage, they knew that neither was going to be happy. Njord longed for the sea and Skadi longed for the mountains. They chose to do what was best for each other and part as friends (more on that relationship in chapter nine).

Developing compassion means being able to be selfless – to practice empathy, to relate to what someone else is going through with kindness and understanding. Being compassionate must start with oneself first! How do you show yourself compassion? Do you comfort yourself? How do you encourage and believe in yourself? Do you?

Living a more mindful day-to-day practice can help increase compassion. When you can disconnect and be present, you can shift your perspective and begin to heal the disconnect with yourself which will make it easier for you to step into a more empathetic way of showing compassion for others.

Even a great huntress and warrior such as Skadi knew when to back down and show honor and because of her loyalty to herself she was able to be more compassionate for Njord.

Conviction is what Skadi displayed when she demanded revenge for her father's death. She showed a "strong belief or opinion" that she was justified. Her father was wrongfully killed and she was going to seek justice. Whether he was wrongfully killed is open to one's interpretation. Thiazi did after all trick Loki into bringing him Idunn, which set about a chain of events that ultimately led to his death.

He too showed conviction in his ownership of Idunn and was willing to fly after Loki to retrieve her no matter the cost. When was the last time you stood up with great conviction? Belief and conviction go hand in hand. What beliefs do you have that you are willing to fight for? Do you have any? It takes great courage to stand up for one's belief with conviction. There are consequences one faces, such as dismissal, rejection or betrayal. There are times though when it is absolutely necessary.

Determination is the main attribute that motivates one to enact all the previous characteristics mentioned. Skadi was determined. Her perseverance, no matter how difficult the task, allowed her to move onward with her quest for vengeance. She was "firm with purpose." She calculated her plan of attack and continued onward.

When was the last time you were determined to do something? My family calls me the "hippie" so naturally when I decided to go into law enforcement there were some comments made. While I honestly cannot tell you why a hippy would go cop, this wasn't even a consideration in my life, I was determined to do it!

My determination consumed me. But I succeeded. If you want to change and experience progression in life then you have to be a bit uncomfortable. Change does not happen when one is complacent. There was no reason or need for me to closet my broom skirts and tie-dye in exchange for pants, boots and a badge (not to mention a bra) but I was determined. I made it a whole two and a half years as a sworn officer before I looked into the mirror and asked myself if I was "determined to keep going even if it meant compromising everything about myself." Well the answer is pretty self-explanatory. My determination served its purpose. There are no regrets with my decision, only gratitude. But clearly I chose writing and priestess service to the goddess over enforcing the law.

Wild by definition is to "live or grow in the natural environment, not domesticated or cultivated; uninhabited, inhospitable." When we use the word wild to describe a person, it can mean "unrestrained, crazy" or "overly enthusiastic." Would you describe yourself as wild? Do you want to?

As a teenager I was wild. Breaking the rules of society and in my opinion rebelling against authority. Is it really wild to do what every other teenager is doing? This is something I ask myself now as an adult. Was I really a wild teenager or just an average teenager doing what teens do?

As an adult I think I am much wilder than I ever was at the age of sixteen, breaking the roles of what society wants me to be and living my life as authentically as I can is to be wild. When I choose to set and honor boundaries, that is me being wild. For all too often I would compromise those boundaries for the comfort of others.

Skadi was deemed wild because she chose to live in the mountains surrounded by wolves rather than in the comfort of the great hall surrounded by people. As a dog-person I totally get this. I would much rather be surrounded by dogs than people. There is a loyalty and companionship with animals that humans are lacking. Maybe we have forgotten that we are mammals too?

For the past two decades I have been anchored into helping clients embrace their wild side and it always comes down to living their most authentic life surrounded by those who are like-minded and want to incorporate the same ideals. When we are around others who live authentically then they mirror to us permission to do just that – live with honor and acceptance of our inner wild.

Think of all the people in your life that you would consider wildly authentic and honor the fact that they are a part of your pack, your loyal friends and like-minded souls that support and encourage each other. If you don't have that in your life then maybe it's time to start living in a way that will magnify and attract it.

Do these characteristics or attributes necessary make Skadi wild? I imagine seeing a Giantess, armed and ready to kill, barging into the great hall and interrupting dinner as one who possesses a wild tenacity. But on their own these attributes are not really "wild" but inspiring. To be so sure of oneself, so determined and so loyal to one's blood that you are willing to risk your life is wildly admirable and something to look to as inspirational.

When I think of being wild, it transports me to 2016 when I attended a goddess festival in the redwood forest of La Honda, Northern California. There is no shy bone in my body! When I am told that this forest is mine and I can run naked and free – I take that quite literally. So there I was running naked on a trail through the redwood forest when I came across some hikers that ... well ... were not naked. What did I do? Well if I was shy I would have kept running while frantically hiding my exposed body from view, but no! I stopped, fully naked and asked them how they were and if they were enjoying this beautiful day? Then I proceeded on with my frolicking. That is wild to me!

When I call to Skadi as a mirror, it is usually when I am lacking in one of these attributes. When I am doubting myself or feeling unsure, I reach out to Skadi. Her attributes are all obtainable! It is also important to honor your individual ideal of any deity. As a mere human, I am more than capable of possessing these attributes that I have attached as the Author to Skadi. I may not have them all at once but they are not unreachable. They are all doable.

We do not have historical facts or documents that confirm any of the old gods. What we have are poems and sagas that were written about 200 years later. We do however have our own desires and thoughts concerning any deity and that is what we should honor. Our focus with interacting and calling upon any deity should be a personal exploration and journey.

A CALL TO SKADI

Standing before your mirror, light a blue or white candle.
Take four deep breaths and anchor into the present moment.

I call to Skadi, great Giantess.
In this moment of self-doubt, I seek to ignite my inner strength and
    conviction.
Will you mirror to me what that looks like?
Will you help me to rise up with confidence?
Will you inspire me to keep going, to not give up?

(Pause and invite her to look to you through the mirror)

Say her name out loud

Close your eyes and breathe in deeply.
Feel your inhale begin to awaken and ignite your highest self.
Focus on your body, your muscles and cells being activated with your
    breath.
Open your eyes and see her as your reflection.
See how strong and confident you really are.
Remember all those times you were energetically knocked down and
    you got back up!
Take a few deep breaths and really look at yourself.
Allow the flame of the candle to illuminate your tenacity.

CHAPTER THREE

Awakening One's Inner Wolf

Is it Skadi's wildness, bravery or tenacity for revenge that makes her so intriguing? Or is it the fact that she prefers the cold of the mountain and the company of wolves? For some, the answer is both, as it rightly should be, but others feel a different pull to work with Skadi. For me, working with a winter snow goddess didn't really offer much appeal. I am not super-fond of winter sports. My idea of skiing is to sit by the fire inside the resort, watch the skiers come down the mountain and sip wine. Snow is beautiful and that first snow storm brings with it an immediate blanket of white calm. But it wasn't so much Skadi that got my attention; rather it was her wolves.

There comes a time in almost everyone's life (especially women where there begins an internal scratching and itch for something more) when there is an overwhelming desire to break free from social norms and gender roles and go running wild with wolves. Something about the wolf stirs this internal itch.

For the past decade I have devoted myself as daughter of the wolf. As an animist witch and shapeshifting priestess, it has been my great honor to lead individuals through shamanic meditation to connection with their spirit animal or as I refer to it in my second book, *The Wheel of the Year with Animals as Guides*, one's primary spirit animal (PSA). When we can disconnect from the mundane realms of our lives and anchor into our own primal, raw and wild mirror of our inner animal then things really begin to shift.

Working with wolf has been my greatest challenge as wolf energy has forced me to act and lead from a space of humility rather than ego. Wolf energy I truly believe is what this world needs in order to create dramatic change and shift the current events. We are living in a world divided, a world anchored into fear, control and power. There is no pack mentality being embraced, it is a world of sheep. Where everyone is being told to follow in order to survive. Scary times, weird times and now more than ever people need to awaken their inner wolf. Find some bravery, wildness and cling to their pack. We have to start somewhere.

There is a myth from the Pueblo people about an old woman named "La Loba". She is a collector of bones, the bones being the essence of one's soul – one's story! Clarissa Pinkola Estes published her book *Women Who Run with the Wolves* in 1992. Since then, a movement of bone collecting women has risen up. There has been an increase in women's empowerment circles and the goddess movement. The story of La Loba is part of that movement.

The inner wolf scratching and the story of La Loba are two of the many instigators in the realm of work that I have been doing since 2003 when I started my first goddess group. A group dedicated to helping women dig up their bones and reclaim their lives. When individuals can gather together without ego and the mean girl archetype then shifts occur and from those shifts permission is mirrored out to everyone that they come into contact with. A confident, powerful "person" is attractively magnetic.

Through the years of goddess/women-only circles, I have learned much that I am grateful for. But circling with only women is not very wolf pack so, as all things in life, a new shift has been embraced. Instead of focusing on just empowering the women, my lover and I have opened up our property and land for everyone to come and circle.

Wolf pack modality is basically the ideal that there is room for more within the pack. Each pack member has their own broken pasts, hurts, wounds and each member of the pack is worthy of a space where they can call to La Loba and reclaim their essence, dig up their bones and start living their most authentic and wild lives with the support of other like-minded souls.

We honor wolf as our totem for the land, and with that we encourage individuals to step up and be the best that they can be in whatever shape they arrive in. Each member of a wolf pack has a vital part to play and without that particular wolf, the pack would be lacking. We strive to accomplish this in our little community here in Southern Utah. With Skadi and La Loba as our wolf mothers watching over us, we strive to help everyone scratch that itch of their inner wolf as it awakens.

LEGEND OF LA LOBA

It is said there is an old woman who lives hidden in the depths of a cave in the mountains of the High Desert. It is said the old woman is weathered, tanned and wrinkled with age, her fingers gnarled and clawed. She is always fat, always hairy and always crouching. It is said the old woman is a crower and a cackler, speaking more animal sounds than human.

She is known by many names and seen by very few.

They call her La Huersa, "Bone Woman".

They call her La Trapera, "Gatherer".

It is said the old woman is a gatherer, a scavenger – a collector of bones.

It is said the old woman searches the dry river beds and hidden canyons seeking out that which has been lost to nature. It is said she gathers the bones and takes them into her cave where she pieces them back together, bone by bone. Reconstructing the skeletons of what once were deer, rattlesnake, rabbit and crow. But her specialty is wolves.

It is said as the old woman places the last bone to complete the skeleton of the wolf that she will crouch down and build a fire. As the fire begins to grow and glow, the bones of the wolf are illuminated. Crouching low over the skeleton, it is said that the old woman asks the bones of the wolf: "What song shall I sing to these bones?"

It is then that soft and low within her womb a song begins to rise up, like a hum. As the old woman sings, the bones of the wolf begin to quiver and quake and the fire begins to grow and the flames grow higher. The old woman sings louder. Soon muscles, tendons, ligaments begin to form upon the bones of the wolf, and the old woman sings louder and the fire grows higher. Soon skin begins to grow on the muscles, tendons and ligaments of the bones of the wolf, and the old woman sings louder!

Her song sounding like wolves howling in the distance.

The fire grows higher, and the desert floor begins to shake!

Fur begins to cover the skin of the muscles, tendons, ligaments and bones of the wolf, as the old woman sings louder! The cave is illuminated by light from the rising flames and the eyes of the wolf open and the wolf runs free from the cave.

It is unknown if it is the sand beneath the paws of the wolf or the Moon shining down from above but as the wolf runs, a shift occurs and from the wolf a wild laughing woman breaks free.

It is said there is an old woman who lives hidden in the depths of a cave in the mountains of the High Desert. It is said she is a crower and cackler, speaking more animal sounds than human.

She is known by many names and seen by very few.

They call her La Loba, "Wolf Woman".

It is said there is a time in every woman's life where she is lost and must wander her inner desert, starving, parched and seeking out *the bones of her life in desperation; she seeks out that which she has lost – that which she has given up. It is said that in these moments of desperation the seeking woman may meet the old woman. She doesn't say much, simply reaches into her satchel, pulling out a bone she offers it to the seeker with one question: "What song will you sing to the bone?"*

It is said there is an old woman who lives hidden in the depths of a cave in the mountains of the High Desert. She is known by many names and seen by very few.

They call her La Loba, "Wolf Woman".

When I share this retelling of the story of La Loba, I often think of Skadi in her mountain home, surrounded by wolves. Skadi and La Loba to me are one and the same. Both offer the companionship, strength and wildness of the wolf. Both offer encouragement to reclaim one's bones and reshape one's own story. Both offer permission to do more, dig more and ultimately be more. Not for anyone else, but for one's own self.

Skadi and La Loba both prefer the safety of their own den and the companionship of the wild – the companionship of animals. Skadi in her home on the mountain and La Loba in her cave in the desert. The story of La Loba is one of my most favorite. After a sharing of her myth, I always asks guests what song will they sing to their bone? What is their bone? If the inner wolf is scratching, how will they itch that? What will make that itch go away and allow the inner wolf to surface?

"A healthy woman is a lot like a wolf: life-giving, inventive, territorially conscious, loyal and loving."

– Clarissa Pinkola Estes.

Awakening one's inner wolf is to awaken that part of you that is wild, untamed and unchained. To awaken the inner wolf is to go back to that time in your life where you buried part of yourself out of shame, guilt, fear or trauma and dig up that bone and reclaim it!

> "We all begin as a bundle of bones lost somewhere in a desert – a dismantled skeleton that lies underneath the sand. It is our work to recover these parts. It is a painstaking process best done when the shadows are just right, for it takes much looking. If we sing the song then we can call up the psychic remains of the wild soul and sing it into vital shape again.
>
> To sing means to use the soul voice. To sing one's truth – one's power. To sing is to breathe soul over what is ailing or in need of restoration. One must descend into a deep mood of great love and feeling until one's desire for relationship with the wild-ish self overflows. Then speak one's soul from that state of mind. That is singing over the bones."
>
> – Clarissa Pinkola Estes.

To awaken one's inner wolf, one must be willing to expand past the approval and validation of others and start by accepting one's full self as whole. This is hard! Especially in a world which spoon-feeds us that acceptance must come from outside of ourselves. Does a wolf wake up in the morning and think "who can I please today" or "what should I do today to make others happy?" No! A wolf wakes up and lives its day fully without compromising who the wolf is.

What are some of wolves attributes? Can you see any of them within yourself? For me, they are mirror reflections of Skadi's attributes: wild, tenacious, confident, strong, compassionate, determined and loyal. If one is lacking confidence, what happened to create that? Are you willing to go back and dig up that bone? Sing its reclamation song?

Life is made of polarities. Light/dark, good/bad, healthy/sick ... you get the idea. We have to have both in order to find balance. Some refer to this work as "shadow work". I refer to it as "wandering the desert". If you have been in a desert you know there is an eerie sense of stillness. The desert is hot, unpredictable and difficult to survive in – just like the top of the mountain is cold, unpredictable and difficult to survive in. But both La Loba and Skadi do just that. They survive in unfavorable living conditions, they seem to prefer it. Are they both embracing their inner wolves and doing deep shadow work? Or have they come to a state of peace, allowance and love?

Often, only when we stop resisting and start shifting our perspectives can we really allow our lives to shift into a more balanced state. When we can accept that both our inner deserts and cold mountains are just a temporary landscape and that they do not determine how we survive or if we thrive, for we are the ones that have to make that decision. Give up, bury our bones or go back, dig them up and sing our reclamation song.

In order to love who you are, you cannot hate the experiences that shaped you.

TIPS TO AWAKEN ONE'S INNER WOLF:

- Embrace the attributes that make you authentic
- Spend more time outdoors – journey into the wilderness
- Honor your pack, elders & lineage
- Develop physical strength
- Challenge yourself often
- Exercise loyalty
- Express your feelings out loud
- Create your own code of conduct and honor it

In this world of comparisons and competition, *embracing attributes that make one authentic* and stand out can be very uncomfortable for some and very liberating for others. It is vital that each person on this planet live their most authentic life, honoring their individual truths and embracing their unique characteristics. All too often we see young people grasping for validation and acceptance and in their efforts to obtain those they compromise their very authentic essence to "fit in". We were not born to conform or fit in. We were all born as unique individuals meant to stand out.

Spending time outdoors allows one to connect with Nature as a vital participant of nature. We are made up of the earth and stars. Get outside! Leave your phone (unless you use it for taking photos), disconnect from the need to surround yourself with noise and listen to the wilderness. Healing can occur rapidly when we leave the mundane hustle and bustle of the chaos and step foot onto a hiking trail, drive up to the mountain and dip our feet in the flowing river. Nature is the greatest healer and teacher.

Part of awakening one's inner wolf has to anchor into where one comes from. Who are you? Who were your ancestors? What trials and struggles did they face? Can you relate to them? One of the most exciting things I did when diving into my DNA was going on a pilgrimage to England and Scotland to discover my ancestral lineages. Wolves *honor the pack, their elders and their lineages*. We can't go back and change our history but we can learn from it. We can honor the sacrifices made. None of us just appeared – we all carry within us a bloodline that carries with it a long history.

Physical strength creates confidence. Being able to physically tackle each task no matter how demanding can be quite rewarding. One doesn't have to spend hours at the gym to become physically strong. Decide on one aspect of your body that you would like to strengthen and devote time and energy into accomplishing that challenge.

In order to grow, we need to be challenged. Often we do not *challenge ourselves* enough because we choose not to. Victimhood and blame has created a society that looks to the Universe as the ultimate challenger, when in actuality we create our universal experience so our reactions to what we experience create the challenges we face. Some are monumental and some are inconsequential, but we are the ones doing the challenges. What if we set the intention to accomplish something new each day? Would this be a challenge worthy of tackling? How would we feel at the end of each day if we really took the time and energy to focus on improvement?

A wolf is *loyal to its pack*. A wolf's very survival depends on the role they play within their pack. Let's face it, we live in a world of boxes where disagreements are not discussed, rather removal, dismissal, blocking and "un-friending" has become the norm. We have people who come into our lives that one minute we love and the next they are disposed of. What if we took the time to really invest in our relationships and work through those disagreements that are worthy of addressing? I love the saying "loyalty is when you have my back, behind my back." How loyal are you? Do you value those in your life that have remained loyal? Chances are yes, but can they say the same thing about you?

There are very few mind-readers on this great sphere some call the Mama. Being able to *express one's feelings without blame or shame* is huge! Not only does this install confidence and personal conviction but it frees one from holding onto feelings that can and usually do create a dis-ease within our physical bodies. Have you ever been super upset and instead of expressing how you felt, you held your tongue and hours later had a sore throat? Our bodies want to filter out the emotions within us but our bodies also need us to release and let go instead of holding onto things. "Anger is like swallowing poison and expecting the other person to die." There are healthy ways of expressing ones feelings and oftentimes, once expressed, the energetic and emotional charge behind those feelings diminishes.

Creating a code of conduct or a day-to-day motto really does help in awakening one's inner wolf. This is a code that you the individual agree to honor and live by each and every day. Remember back when the book *The Secret* by Rhonda Byrne came out and everyone was writing down affirmations and shifting their dialogue to be more positive? What happened to that? For me, a code of conduct amps up the power of affirmations because they become a commitment, promise and a vow that one makes each and every day.

Skadi to me is a wild wolf woman! Mother of Wolves! She encompasses all the qualities of one who has truly awakened her inner wolf enough that she is more comfortable surrounded by other wolves. Think of those people in your life that you would consider wolves. What characteristics or attributes do they have that you admire?

While doing so, please disconnect from the negative view of wolves. We have been mislead for centuries to believe that wolves are aggressive and fierce. We have been spoon-fed the image of an "alpha" leading based purely on fear and intimidation. In fact, wolves are not fiercely aggressive. The model of the alpha is incredibly outdated and misinformed. There is no alpha in the wolf pack, there is a mother and father who birthed the pack and ensured its survival. Think of your parents, would you refer to them as "alphas"?

Skadi was part of the pack, not leader of the pack. She protected her pack just like they protected her. Think of all the things a pack provides ... warmth, security, protection, companionship, loyalty. Do you have a pack? If not, what can you do to start creating one? Any time a community is formed, there is a natural hierarchy – has that hierarchy been clearly defined? Is there a family feel where parents are leading or is there one at the top that seeks power, dominion and control? If it is the latter then you may want to rethink this pack and your role within it.

When I look at my own pack, my family, which consists of my parents, siblings, children, nieces, nephews, cousins, aunts, uncles, dear friends and grandchildren; there is not anyone who owns the pack, rules the pack or dictates how we as individuals live. It is my opinion that my parents succumbed to having control over any of us wild-lings long ago. Within my pack there is love, respect and devotion. When someone has a need, we all reach out to help. There is no seniority, no dominance, no aggression and certainly no alpha!

There are levels within a pack, these levels are established by years of experience, time and service rendered. For example, when Papa says something in a certain tone, everyone in the pack stops what they are doing and listens. Is this out of fear or aggression? No! The eldest of the pack leads the pack. Just like the mother of the pack birthed the pack and without her there would be no pack, so there is a natural level of respect given freely.

With time comes progression, and with progression comes change. In order to change and be fluid in any group, there needs to be adaptability and patience as everyone within the pack shifts and grows individually with the hopes to grow collectively. To be in a pack is not a solo gig! There can't be a good stew with only one ingredient. In a pack the "more" really is the merrier – if everyone in the pack is responsible for their individual selves bettering the majority, then the pack will survive. If there are people in the pack only focused on their success at the demise of the pack, then the pack is doomed and never was a pack to begin with.

CHAPTER FOUR

Eradicating the Lone Wolf Archetype

In the spring of 2021, I invited fifteen women to stay on my property and devote a weekend to "Running with Wolves." The intention was to activate wolf pack. To do this we lived together as a pack, ate all meals together and participated fully in classes, rituals and activities. In the opening circle it was made clear that there would be zero tolerance for the *lone wolf*. That archetype that is so falsely idolized was not welcome at this weekend.

A lone wolf is a sick wolf, a sick wolf is a dying wolf. A lone wolf is a dead wolf! In an actual wolf pack, a lone wolf has either been exiled from the pack due to a very serious violation of the pack code (can you imagine doing something so horrendous that your family excuses you?) or that wolf is sick, dying and does not wish to contaminate the others.

This exiled wolf will not wander for long. A wolf cannot survive on its own. So this wolf will search for another pack and have to earn its keep through some pretty serious trials starting from the bottom and groveling for acceptance. Wolves do not and will not isolate by choice.

The lone wolf archetype that we see embraced so heavily is inaccurate and portrays the wolf in a negative light. In my line of work as priestess and one that offers community events almost weekly, I have seen a variety of people come and go. When in discussion with new comers, our intention of our space is devoted to wolf pack. There have been a few people who often reply with: "I am a lone wolf." this statement lets me know that this individual is unwilling to embrace community and pack mentality. They are simply above such things, riding ego and arrogance and they prefer to be alone. These people very rarely come back for a second visit.

We spent this entire weekend as a pack. When a woman would pull away and feel like she needed to isolate, there would always be others who would remind her: "You are not a lone wolf." This has become a chant that offers security and a reminder that no one is really alone unless they push their pack away.

> "The strength of the pack is the wolf and the strength of the wolf is the pack."
>
> – Rudyard Kipling

In an article on *lonerwolf.com* (ironically) it states that: "Archetypes are omnipresent. They are within you, they are within others and they create the very foundation of human behavior." These archetypes are behaviors and energies that we as individuals display and show to the world, whether intentionally or not. You can even take an online test to determine what archetype is dominant within you. The archetype of the lone wolf is counter-productive to growth as it encourages ego, isolation and the motion that one does not need anyone else.

When I have a client or guest express to me that they are a *lone wolf*, my response is usually: "Well, it's good your mother wasn't a lone wolf or you would not be here." As a society, we need to break this cycle of being alone as being empowered! Isolation is unhealthy. We witnessed in our society in a mere two years of the Covid pandemic a rise in mental illness, depression and suicide. Why was this? We were forced into isolation! People were removed from family and died alone. Now things have progressed and the medical field has now allowed Covid patients to have visitors because they saw firsthand that isolation made thing worse!

Our mental and physical health are intertwined. Without the stimulation of social interactions, loneliness creeps in along with depression, anxiety and suicidal tendencies. "Feeling safe and protected is a fundamental primary need of the human being to be able to move freely in the surrounding world, as well as the feeling of having control over the events in our own lives. When all this fails, when the belief that whatever we do will not improve, things begins to develop – a sense of "learned helplessness" takes hold, blocking any possibility of liberation or change."

https://www.frontiersin.org/articles/10.3389/fpsyg.2020.02201/full

We are pack oriented! No one is born alone. It's not natural to isolate. It's certainly not wolf pack. To increase and improve mental health, we need to interact with others. Social interaction is good for one's brain. When we have a pack that we can talk to and spend time with, we feel a sense of belonging, security and we can confide in others and create a space where others can confide in us. This is healthy!

When a person isolates, they cut off contact, avoid physical touch and crawl into their den to achieve what? The mere act of touch from another stimulates the feel-good hormone oxytocin. This hormone (often called the love hormone, cuddle hormone or bonding hormone) is vital! When oxytocin is released, dopamine and serotonin are also released, which reduces stress and we feel good. In the pack there is always some kind of non-sexual physical touch. A pack person is a happy person. A happy person is a healthy person.

Skadi is not lacking interaction. She is part of a pack and she mirrors to us the importance of pack mentality and health.

We need others in our lives. While I understand first-hand that humans are the cruelest predator on the planet, we still need each other. But it's okay if one prefers the companionship of animals over people – those people are still embracing pack mentality, just with other species. Like Skadi, who was invited to live amongst the gods (she even married one of them) – her home, security and sense of belonging were found in the wild amongst wolves.

This lone wolf archetype is unhealthy and damaging to society. Now, more than ever, we need each other. What is beautiful is that now, as this pandemic is in its third year, we are seeing more and more a shift towards encouragement of gatherings, families coming together and visitors allowed into the hospital to be with the sick. When my best friend's father was sick with pneumonia following Covid, he was in the hospital for almost two weeks and his children, spouse and grandchildren were with him every day up until he died from heart complications. When I spoke to my friends, they both expressed how grateful they were and how grateful their father was that they could be together. We need interactions! We need to connect. We need to uplift, encourage, challenge and listen to each other.

We need to eradicate from our psyche this weird desire to be on our own, to do things ourselves and to prove that to whomever that we can. Why do we do this? It's so foreign to me. As an independent person who has spent my whole life swimming against the current of what society has told me a woman should be, my drive and determination was never out of spite or to prove something to others. My drive and determination was for me. I can be strong, independent and still be part of a pack. The same goes for everyone!

A true pack will celebrate the individual and not expect them to conform. Wolf pack modality honors that each wolf serves a purpose and that the pack as a whole would be lacking if not for that wolf. We each have something to offer, we each have gifts, unique abilities and profound truths. What good are they if we cannot share them? If we cannot recognize these attributes in others and allow individuals to shine and not feel threatened then we are doomed as a society.

This "dog-eat-dog world" (which is actually contradictory to how dogs really are) is a phrase that encourages individuals to do whatever it takes to be successful, even at the expense of others. Humans have become cruel and selfish which only feeds into this lone wolf madness. Capitalist societies are dog-eat-dog societies where each individual is encouraged to look out for their own self-interest before the interest of others and certainly before the interests of their community.

Is it possible to shift this modern day embraced concept? Is it possible to eradicate the lone wolf? Yes! For starters, if we as individuals can embrace the Dalai Lama's advice and be more mindful, selfless and compassionate with ourselves then we can naturally mirror that to others. We can see that yes we can be individuals, we can allow others to be individuals and we can come together as a pack and then society will begin to reap the benefits of being unified.

Maybe if we stopped fighting over silly things, making harmful comparisons and ended the patriarchal urge to compete we could start living as a unified pack!

Scientists have stated that "wolves are essential in solving the imbalance of the environment as a whole." How can we, as humans, help? Are we capable of emulating and mirroring within our social constructs wolf pack modality? Can we truly live together harmoniously and still remain individuals?

What is a wolf pack? In the incredible must-read book, *The Wisdom of Wolves* by Jim & Jamie Dutcher, they describe a wolf pack as being "a tribe, a clan, a family, a confederacy. They are also an assembly of individual personalities, private desires and goals and inner lives largely unknown. They are individuals, each with his or her way of being and interacting with the others. They are social and they need each other. Wolves have evolved to live and function within a society."

A lone wolf archetype or personality cannot survive within a pack because they do not honor the pack. They see themselves as above and superior. In other words, lone wolf people choose distance rather than alliance within a league. This is choice! This is something that we are being spoon-fed by society – that we do not need each other, live and let die, eye for an eye and dog-eat-dog. This type of mindset only creates division.

Within a wolf pack, each wolf knows who they are, what their role is and that they are vital to the pack, and the survival of the pack depends on each wolf fulfilling their individual role to their best abilities. Together as a pack they care for each other's needs. The elders are honored and fed by the young. The pups are raised by the pack and when another wolf is sick or injured, each wolf within the pack takes turns caring for that wolf. Wolves care for each individual and when one dies the entire pack grieves and mourns that loss, for it is truly a loss. Do we see this in society?

Trust is the key ingredient and that to me is why we are seeing within our human society the increase of the lone wolf archetype. We as humans have lost trust in one another and rightly so. Within a wolf pack trust is vital. Erik Ziman, a wolf expert, stresses that trust is the most important ingredient in the formation of a safe and healthy pack.

Simply put – an individual wolf wants to belong to a pack, whereas humans are losing that desire to belong altogether. Betrayal, competition, disagreements and dictating leaders are making the concept of living alone, isolated away from all the chaos a much more appealing possibility.

While the lone wolf archetype is filled with misinformation and false perceptions on life being better alone and the strength of not needing anyone the *alpha* archetype has also led us mere humans astray. We have been taught that alpha wolves are aggressive and fought their way to the top. This is completely false! Being an alpha wolf has absolutely nothing to do with aggression but everything to do with responsibility. "Those who birthed the pack naturally rule the pack." This is not out of control or with ferociousness but rather parenting hierarchy. An alpha wolf is defined as the "one who patrols the boundaries of their territory looking for danger. They are keepers of pack knowledge. They are assured, alert and compassionate. A true alpha is a leader in the very best sense. Protecting the pack is the alphas solemn duty." Do we see this kind of leadership within our communities? Probably not!

In *The Wisdom of Wolves* book, the lone wolf archetype is described as a "person who acts alone, cares for no one and craves no companionship. In Nature, a lone wolf is a temporary phenomenon, what biologists call a "disperser". What does a lone wolf in the wild want? It wants to stop being a lone wolf! It wants togetherness, to be part of something bigger. Survival depends on it. As much as we as humans admire individual prowess, we are only as good as our collective effort. Wolves need each other just as humans need each other."

Let's collectively eradicate this lone wolf archetype. We humans are social creatures. We enjoy being around each other, working together and together we can accomplish so much more than if we were working the same task alone. Remember the old English proverb: "Many hands make light work." The very first civilizations operated in a similar fashion to a wolf pack. They worked together to ensure their survival. We can get back to that modality.

Hosting a three day, three night event is not an easy task. However, when every individual understands that they are respected as individuals and required to participate fully, things shift. Not everyone within a pack, circle, tribe, clan or family gets along all of the time. That is a very unhealthy and unrealistic expectation or rather daydream. When disagreements or tension erupt within a group, we have an opportunity to grow as a group. We can agree to disagree and still be respectful.

For the past six years, it has been my privilege and challenge to bring women together for these weekends. It's not easy! But when I see women working together, caring for each other, cooking together, cleaning up together and appreciating each other as individuals then there is an undeniable feeling that a pack, clan, tribe, sisterhood and family is forming. It is a beautiful thing to see people coming together as strangers and leaving as family.

WAYS TO ERADICATE THE LONE WOLF ARCHETYPE

- Stop viewing others as competition.
  - When we compare ourselves to others, when we covet and crave what someone else has, we enter a state of competition.
  - When we compare, we compete and when we compete we defeat.

- Learn to agree to disagree!
  - Stop demanding that others see things from your perspective. This is unhealthy and unrealistic.
  - Stop wasting time and energy demanding that everyone you surround yourself with think, act and believe the way you do. Where is the variety and individuality?

- Learn to love and allow others to surface their individuality.
  - Remember that every flower, even of the same species, is unique and individual. Let the people in your life show up as they are and who they are.

- Volunteer!
  - When people work together, magic happens.
  - Find a church, group or organization and volunteer some time and energy.

- Communicate eye-to-eye and heart-to-heart.
  - Put down your phone!
  - When you sit face-to-face with someone and really communicate, free from distraction, that is how relationships, friendships and packs are formed. Listen without responding.

- Show up for those in need.
  - Honor the elders in your community. Offer assistance when you can. This can be simply taking back a shopping cart for an elder or opening a door. When someone is sick, offer to be of assistance. You can do more than just send energy and love from afar. We need to start taking care of each other.

- Celebrate others accomplishments!
  - Be happy for someone when they succeed. Cheer them on! Congratulate them!

Remember that Skadi chose to live amongst the gods and still periodically return home to her mountain and wolves. You too can be part of a community, circle, group, clan, tribe, coven or pack and still return home to your private space and individual pack. You can do both!

While eradicating the lone wolf archetype is vital to our growth as a society in reclaiming pack mentality, we must also eradicate or shift our perspective on another archetype; that being the Ice Queen. You all know her. Stone cold, hostile, void of empathy, compassion, a forceful person who has made it known that they do not work well with others unless those others are bowing down to them.

The term archetype stems from ancient Greek with its root words being *archein* meaning "original/old" and *typos* meaning "pattern/type". Carl Gustav Jung, a psychologist, believed that "Universal, mythic characters and archetypes reside within the collective unconscious of people all over the world.

These archetypes represent fundamental human motifs of our experience as we evolved." In other words, archetypes represent personality traits.

There are literally hundreds of archetypes. Since Skadi is also known as the Ice Queen, it seems fitting to address the somewhat negative, shadow, darker aspect of this title. Archetypes are embraced! Personality traits are fed by the individual. What is amazing is our ability to adapt, and with adaptation comes growth. So even though we may be embracing a certain archetype or personality trait, we do have the ability to outgrow that, shift and change.

Who are the Ice Queens in your life? By definition the Ice Queen archetype is fearsome; she possesses a frosty, icy or wintry personality which makes her unapproachable. She, like the lone wolf, is often without friends or a pack. Why? Most likely because she is a stone cold bitch. Let's face it, we all know people like this – ruthless, cold, demanding, disrespectful, contemptuous.

Ice Queens are known to be narcissists. Those who display this trait are usually too good for anyone. As queens, however, they do appreciate followers and devotees who serve them through adoration. Think of Margaret Thatcher, the former British Prime Minister who was rightfully referred to as the *Iron Lady*. Even the Snow Queen in the Hans Christian Andersen fable was fiercely unkind, possessing a frozen heart which made her incapable of compassion.

While Ice Queens are usually very beautiful on the outside; inside they are aching, hurt, and they cover up their extreme pain and loneliness by being cruel. With a fake smile they appear to listen to what you are saying, while in their mind they are dismissing you on every level. Oh! We have all met the Ice Queens. Maybe we have been an Ice Queen to others?

It is my belief that this persona is embraced out of self-defense and self-preservation, almost as if cruelty becomes a shield and armor against being hurt. See, the Ice Queen archetype doesn't just happen overnight. As with all archetypes, life's events and experiences help shape us into who we are. Every Ice Queen I have met is hurting deep down and they are not willing to be hurt again. So they put up a wall. They display a RBF (resting bitch face). They make themselves intimidating and unapproachable because if they can keep people at a distance then they cannot be hurt.

What is intimidating about the Ice Queens is that they have developed a lone wolf belief that they do not need anyone. No outside person is going to fill any void. A true Ice Queen is very intelligent, successful and independent – one who is beyond comfortable with her solitary life.

We see depictions of Ice Queens as female villains. We are taught that these strong powerful, independent women are evil, possessing bad qualities. In the TV show *Game of Thrones*, we see Cersei, played by Lena Headey, as the evil queen – the villain. Yet there is something about her strength, her conviction and her power that is attractive. In the show *American Horror Story*, we see Jessica Lange portray Fiona Goode the "baddest witch" – another powerhouse.

Even in the wolf pack, the female leader will turn a bit icy and cold towards the pack weeks before she gives birth to pups. She has better things to do and focus on than be involved with the day-to-day of the pack. It is fairly common for her to distance herself physically and emotionally.

When it comes to eradicating the Ice Queen, most women will object and resist, which is understandable. Being the doe-eyed princess is not attractive either – just like in the myth of Skadi, where she chooses her mountain home and wolves, yet she can return to realm of the gods and walk amongst them accepted as a goddess; we too can be a bit icy in order to self-preserve and yet still be part of the pack. It all comes down to balance, which comes with healing.

If you really look at your own life, do some self-realization and see how you have allowed things to shape you then you will know there are ebbs and flows, highs and lows. We all have trauma, pain, heartache and frustrations. We can shape these into something fearsome and cruel which would prevent us from having to experience those again, or we can shift our perspective and own our reactions, which would ultimately bring us into self-accountability.

Don't get me wrong, I do not loathe all the Ice Queens. Some I do and some I don't. Cersei and Fiona Goode were the only reasons I watched Game of Thrones and American Horror Story. These women are powerful, raw and primal. Skadi is powerful, raw and primal and if I was to run into her dressed in her leather and furs, armed for battle then I would be very intimated by her and probably steer clear.

There is much to learn from both the lone wolf and the Ice Queen. Time and place is something that everyone needs to acknowledge, understand and embrace. There is a time when a lone wolf must leave the pack and wander in the hopes of being embraced by another pack. There is a time when an Ice Queen must bare some teeth and have no mercy.

When one's goal is to empower oneself, there are other ways to do so that do not encourage the Regina George archetype (from the movie *Mean Girls*) to surface. We all struggle with expectations that are forced upon us as children, in relationships, the workplace, by society. We can learn to take our weaknesses and shift them into strengths without using aggressive tactics.

The mean girl is an archetype that I have dealt with my entire life. At times, I too have played the role. We do this for many reasons and it can be consuming, even wasteful. Skadi was an Ice Queen loathed and hated by those who wronged her because she let them know she would not tolerate that behavior.

Look at Loki. Skadi and Loki were entwined together by fate and choice. Loki was responsible for Skadi's father's death.

Skadi was responsible for avenging her father's death. This was accepted by both, yet Loki made her laugh, creating a temporary pause in their fateful hate. At the end of it all, when Loki was finally punished for his many crimes against the gods, it was Skadi who would place the poisonous snake that would spit painful venom into Loki's face. Loki was known as Father of Wolves and Skadi Mother of Wolves. These two were bound, but they also made choices along the way and that was to pause their reactions, even if only temporarily.

We have choices to bind ourselves to life's experiences that have created archetypes that most of us are happy to relate to OR we can let those archetypes surface as needed. There is a time to retreat, tuck oneself into one's den and embrace isolation. There is a time to stand in one's power and not bow down – asserting dominance and displaying strength.

Let's eradicate the need to anchor into one archetype as the only one. This behavior only leads to "my way is the only way" thinking. It's unhealthy and it prevents us from expanding and growing as individuals. You could get online today and take a dozen archetype personality quizzes and each day get a new result. That's how it should be! We are constantly in a state of change. Each day is a new beginning and each day we are faced with choices that will shape the overall outcome of that day. When we anchor into one box that defines us, we are only limiting ourselves.

CHAPTER FIVE

Mother of Wolves

Mother of Wolves is another one of the many titles attached to Skadi. This one in particular could have many reasons behind it. It's safe to speculate, since we really do not have concrete evidence that her attachment and companionship with wolves was factual. There could be many reasons why she was given the title of mother.

In our lives, we are all mothers to ourselves, regardless of assigned gender or chosen life roles. The definition of mother is: "One who gives birth or has the responsibility of physical and emotional care for specific offspring." The undeniable truth is that all humans come from a mother. We were all once infants, children, teenagers and then adults. As adults, we do not have someone to care for us, nurture us and provide for our needs like our mothers did when we were small. Instead we must fulfill those tasks on our own, we must mother ourselves. Each new day is a new start, a blank page and it's up to us as individuals to birth or create what our day will be like.

When Skadi's marriage with Njord failed and they divorced (which will be discussed in greater depth in a later chapter), it is said that Skadi married Odin and bore him many sons. Odin too is depicted with wolves. Could this title of *Mother of Wolves* be describing the sons of Odin and Skadi?

In a wolf pack, the female wolf who births the pack is the matriarch – she is leader, she has power. This mother wolf will spend months preparing for the birth of her pups, along with the help of her mate and the entire pack. Once her den is complete, she will not allow anyone, even her mate, to go inside.

The arrival of pups is a big deal within a wolf pack, for it ensures the survival of the pack. When it comes time for the pups to arrive, the mother wolf is typically alone, unless she has assigned a female wolf to accompany her. Mother wolves, like human mothers, are very instinctual, intuitive and fiercely protective. Once the pups are born, the mother wolf will stay with them for several weeks, devoting all her time, energy and attention to ensuring their survival.

As a mother of three children, two of which were born at home, I can honestly say that being a mother of other human beings is the hardest thing I have ever chosen to do. Mothers sacrifice much to bring babies into this world. We give up our bodies for nine months, enduring muscle aches, weight gain, and hormone shifts that can be very frightening and then when the time comes to give birth; mothers walk the line between life and death. Birth can be scary.

When I was heavily engrossed in birthing and raising my three children, I started apprenticing as a midwife and attending births. This was a very profound time in my life. My days became a juggling act and oftentimes I was depleted by the end of the day, only to be woken up in the middle of the night to assist at a birth. Babies do not come at convenient times. It has been my privilege to attend over 30 births in my short midwifery career and each birth was like walking on holy ground. There is a magic that takes place and one cannot help but stand in awe at the power of mothers.

Instinct! That's what the magic is. A woman's body knows what to do when labor comes. That is why she has a cervix and uterus! Contractions of the uterus happen because the body knows what to do – it is designed to birth. I have seen women resist out of fear what is happening within their bodies and I have seen women trust the process. Each birth is unique and powerful. Animals too can birth with ease or with complications. The difference is that an animal knows it must rely purely on its instincts. There is no doula or nurse telling an animal to breathe. No outsider is "coaching" the mother animal on how to birth – she just gives birth. Birth is a natural process and the body knows what to do.

Mother wolves are excellent mirrors of instincts. They show us as humans how to get out of our own way and trust the process. Remember that trust is the key to wolf pack survival. Skadi as *Mother of Wolves* shows us how to be strong, diligent and never give up. She is the ultimate mirror of one who is whole, wild and lets her instincts lead the way. Honestly, this is easier said than actually done, but that is where determination comes into play.

There is a challenge to mothering though. Each child is born as a unique individual with unique needs. What works for one won't necessarily work for another. As a mother, one must maintain a gracious flow and allow oneself to learn as they grow. The same is true for wolves. No two pups are the same! No two wolves the same.

When my babies were young, I thought that I excelled at being a mother. Now that they are adults, looking back I often feel like a failure. Being a mother of adult children is incredibly hard. Adults make their own decisions and as parents we don't have much say or input. We become observers. While I cried tears of exhaustion when my children were small, now I cry tears of frustration. With being an adult comes adult consequences and as a mother, as a parent, the last thing we want is for our children to learn the hard way.

My dear sister once told me, after I vented to her about the frustrations of being a parent to my adult children, that "being a mother is heart-rending. Oftentimes our children take us for granted, using us as their emotional punch-bags because we are the only ones that they know will always love them and never leave them." This spoke volumes to me. Even within a wolf pack, there are trials and struggles. With no wolf being the same as another and each wolf possessing its own unique personality, I am sure that being a mother wolf is not a walk in the park.

There is a saying that "it takes a village to raise a child." Well, it takes a pack to raise a wolf. The beauty of a wolf pack is that every wolf within the pack helps in the raising of the pups – from the time those pups first leave their den, all the other wolves stand guard. It is the entire pack that teaches the young wolves how to hunt, eat and work together. This is true for us humans as well, whether we see it or not. It really does take a village.

In our adult lives, it still takes a village! Think of your circle of people, your family, tribe, clan, coven, pack or community. Write down each person's name and write down which role/s they fulfill. Who is the mother of your pack? Who is the father? What roles do they play? Our social skills within our individual circles and communities create our survival within those structures. We know who is in our circles and we know the roles that they play. We too play a role. Now think of one of those pack members leaving, there is a void left behind, especially when that individual fulfilled their role to their fullest. When we participate fully in our lives and our circles, everyone feels it.

When a wolf decides to leave its pack, whether it's a violation and is excused or whether it's to ensure the survival of the species by finding another pack, there is a time period of wandering. That lone wolf surfaces and with it comes loss and feelings of being lonely. We have all been there; we have all felt that period of being alone. Feeling the loss of what was once a safe circle or pack to now the unknown. As mother, it must be hard to watch this upheaval, even though it is vital to the individual wolf's survival, it is sad to witness. There is a mourning period that happens both within the wolf pack and within our human packs.

When our children moved out of our house, there was joy, excitement and worry. Oftentimes, I would feel sad at the end of the day as I walked past their room and they were not there to say good night to. Many nights were restless from worrying if they were safe and making smart decisions. The weight a mother carries is heavy.

Strength is something that I look to in Skadi when it comes to mothering. Seeing the wild in her wolves and letting them run free allows me to apply that perspective to my now adult children. In the book, *The Wisdom of Wolves* by Elli H. Radinger, there is a whole chapter dedicated to seeing the mirror between wolves and women/mothers. "Mothers are the true centre of the family. The leaders in a group are the ones who suffer the most stress. They have a responsible position that involves long-term, high social stress. It is the mother who must maintain harmony within the pack by setting out clear tasks and boundaries. Some alpha females come from a long line of leading personalities. Very often, the daughters of leading mothers also become leaders of the pack. They learn it from their mothers."

What is the role of Mother Wolf? Well, she is the one who ensures the survival of the pack by keeping them together and instilling harmony and balance. Do mother wolves make mistakes? Absolutely! Just like humans. As a mother, I have done much right and much wrong (depending on the day and which child you talk to). Mothers get tired, frustrated and are not always the best mirrors or examples of patience, harmony and pristine poise. Mother wolves nip, bite and bark at their pups. This is where that village and pack comes into play with the *"many hands make light work."* Well, many paws make light the work as well.

Skadi is the cover girl, cover goddess for all things wild woman! Ethnologist and psychoanalyst, Clarissa Pinkola Estes, is well known her belief that: *"In every woman a wolf-woman slumbers, the guardian of the female primal instincts and intuitive knowledge of right and wrong. A woman can only be strong, healthy, creative, whole and happy when she gets back to the root of her instinctive nature: the wolf-woman, the wild, untamed primal woman within her."* There is an aching in all of us, regardless of assigned gender, to be more wild and untamed. Skadi shows us how! In essence, we can consider each of us her wolves and she our mother.

Naturally as pups, teenagers and adults we resist anyone with any kind of authority. Even our own mothers we reject, resist and push away. There is no greater relationship than that of mother and child. Even energetically, we push back against our own tendencies to mother ourselves.

Every day is filled with choices that we are the ones responsible to make. Sometimes we are more instinctual and other times we ride ego and weigh the pros and cons. Ultimately, though, we are one-hundred percent accountable for how our day begins and ends. This is a hard concept to grasp for those who have learned to embrace the role of victim. Some of us still buy into the negative concept that being wild is simply not a possibility.

In these times where we doubt our strengths and we forget that we are a part of nature and as such nature has its own timing, we can call to Skadi; not only for her wisdom prowess as mother but also her pack of wolves to remind us that within us all there is a wolf energy that sometimes needs to be woken up. "Wolves follow the rhythm of life: they hunt, eat, reproduce and look after their families. They do what all living creatures do in nature: they celebrate the here and now."

From the time we are children we are asked: "what do you want to be when you grow up?" This mindset of focusing on the future and creating a narrative of goals that we will achieve and manifest while healthy can also pull us so far away from the present that we forget altogether how to live in the present and enjoy the little things. We become obsessed with setting intentions and creating and planning what the week will hopefully be that we forget about this moment, this hour and this day.

Animals are the gods that walk amongst us. They are constantly teaching us and really they are constantly mothering us, if we will accept their guidance and nurturing. Wolves have so much to teach us and their wise ways show us how we as humans can evolve and come together to bring about harmony and balance. Yet we resist their teachings and we embrace our human role as the greatest predator on the planet. Only, instead of eradicating the wolves, we will eradicate our humanity because we insist on hunting and killing our inner wild.

Centuries ago, the common belief was that wolves were dangerous, wild and aggressive monsters. "The only good wolf was a dead wolf." While this mindset has shifted and been deemed ignorant, the majority of humans struggle to learn from the wolf. Rather there are some who are focused on controlling the wild wolf within and around us, both in the wilderness and in our communities. If we could learn from the Mother of Wolves and care for, nurture and protect each other as all wolves from the same pack then maybe things can shift? Maybe…?

There is a legend I wish to share with you – it is said that a wise Cherokee Elder was once teaching his grandchild about life. "There is a war going on inside of me," said the Elder, "it is a war between the two wolves."

He continued, "One wolf is evil. He is anger, envy, sorrow, jealousy, regret, greed, arrogance, self-pity, guilt, resentment, lies, false pride, ego. But the other wolf is good. He is joy, peace, love, hope, serenity, humility, kindness, benevolence, truth, empathy, generosity, compassion and faith."

Then the Elder placed a hand upon the shoulder of his grandchild. "This same war is raging within you and within the heart of every man, woman and child," he said. The grandchild was thoughtful for a minute and then he asked, "Which wolf will win?"

The Elder's reply was simple, "The one you feed."

I have learned that the point of life's walk is not where or how far I move my feet but how I am moved in my heart. If I walk far but am angry toward others as I journey, I walk nowhere.

If I conquer mountains but hold grudges against others as I climb, I conquer nothing. If I see much but regard others as enemies, I see no one.

Whether we walk among our people or alone among the hills, happiness and life's walking depends on how we feel about others in our hearts. We travel only as far and as high as our hearts will take us.

If I was to move forward, I needed to leave all that was backward behind, whatever you carry that invites a backward walking – leave it behind.

Which wolf will win? The one you feed.

– Anasazi Foundation youtube video

As a mother, I have shared this Cherokee legend with my own children many times. There is within us two wolves and we are the ones who feed them. Sometimes the *evil* one may lie dormant for many years until it awakens and is fed with our reactions. Sometimes this evil one is only resting for a few hours before it is fed. Sometimes we become imbalanced by only feeding the *good* one. The key really is trusting the process and seeing the wolves in others. It comes down to our self-accountability and our reactions. This is hard for many, myself included!

Make no mistake; we are very much like wolves. We are living breathing creatures with our very unique, individual personalities. We have a soul. We are intelligent, persistent, loyal and emotional. We are capable of adapting and surviving. Oftentimes we make life harder than it needs to be because we try to force things rather than allow things to happen in their own time. We forget to play and focus on the future while missing out on the present.

Pack mentality is vital! Without it we would have no one. We would be wandering lost and lonely. As a priestess, it is my honor to offer service to my community, which is why my lover and I built the Utah Goddess Temple. We wanted to create a den where those seeking a pack could gather, celebrate and expand. Our goal the past two years has been to emulate wolf pack modality. Through the years we have seen many people come and people go. Some have stayed and some just couldn't handle the responsibility of being a part of something greater than themselves.

When I was ordained and given the title Lady Wolf in the mountains of the Red Wood Forest by Zsuzusanna Budapest, I knew that I was being given responsibilities, not elevation. As such, I take these responsibilities very seriously. I've dedicated my life to honoring the wolves, not just within my pack and community but in the world around me. Skadi has been my role-model and oftentimes my greatest challenger. It's easy to say you will do something; it's another thing to actually do it.

Skadi is both one of the pack and leader of the pack. She is Mother of Wolves. One can argue that or one can defend that. Rather than waste time doing both, why not allow yourself to awaken the wolf within? Be the wolf; know which wolf you will feed.

There is no greater love than that of a mother. Not all mothers are created equal but in life we tend to find mother figures that help us fill certain voids. We cannot deny the mother archetype, for without her we would not exist – literally! When it comes to mothers, we need to honor the sacrifice that they made to house us within them; this is the beginning of their protective instincts.

Mothers are powerful, but they are not perfect. This is something that I struggle with daily. As a daughter, my relationship with my own mother has been rocky. There were many times where I didn't like my mother and I knew she did not like me. But at the core, we both loved each other. When I am hurting and feeling discouraged, it is still my mother that I call. Even if I do not like her advice, she is the one that I return to again and again. With my own children, I can see the pattern; they come to me with needs, hurts and woes. I am sure that they do not always appreciate my advice or comfort, as their eye-rolling confirms their annoyance.

Mother wolves engage so much time and energy into preparing for their pups and the birthing process can be quite difficult on many levels. They remain steadfast and present. Skadi as Mother of Wolves is steadfast and present. There when you need her. But she will not do the work for you, no one will. Skadi to me is a firm mother. Not really someone I go to when I need cuddles or compassion but rather one I call to when I need a good quick nip, bark and a bite to remind me that I know better. How will you call upon Skadi?

PRAYER TO THE MOTHER OF WOLVES

Great Skadi
I call to you.
In a time when I am weighted down
with woes, frustrations and sorrows.

Mother of Wolves
lend me some strength.
Help me to trust my instincts instead
of questioning them.

Mother of Wolves
lend me patience.
Help me to be still, quiet my mind
that I may enter the present moment.

Mother of Wolves
lend me comfort.
Help me to remember that I am not alone,
that my pack is nearby.

Mother of Wolves
please hear my howling cry.
As your pup I call to you.

There are wolf mothers that have been mentioned throughout myths and legends that are responsible for saving, raising and helping populate the notion that we humans are descendants of wolves, which is why we crave connection with them.

Rome was founded by Romulus and Remus – two twin babies that were tossed into the river in their cradle, doomed to die until the she-wolf "Lupa" saved them, nursed them and cared for them until they were safe. Lupa is revered as Wolf Mother of Rome. Wolves are honored in Rome as symbols of fierce bravery.

There is a legend of another boy who survived a great battle and was injured. He was found by a she-wolf "Asena" who nursed him back to health and kept him safe from his enemies. This boy later mated with the wolf which became pregnant and gave birth to ten half-human/half-wolf sons who would become rulers of the ancient Turkish Nomadic Tribes.

Genghis Khan was thought to have been born of both a deer and a wolf. He credits wolves for being the reason he was so successful in battles, as he learned all his hunting methods by observing wolves hunt their prey.

Society needs to understand that wolves are not fierce aggressive predators. They do not spend their days stalking humans to attack them. They are focused on their own family units. In movies, wolves are often painted in a very negative light, apex predators being their main defining feature. What they fail to state in movies is why are the wolves predators, why are they attacking. Are they defending their family? Do they have pups that that are protecting? Has another predator come into their territory or den?

Human mothers and wolf mothers have much in common. Both spend ample amount of time preparing for the arrival of their young. Both devote time and energy feeding, caring for and raising their young. The difference is that humans tend to do this on their own with just one mate and wolves have an entire pack that assists in the raising, care and protection of the young. In order for the wolf pack to survive, the pups have to survive.

Wolf mothers also are very compassionate and will help raise other wolves' pups. If something happens to the mother, another female wolf will step in, feed the pups and care for them. Again, wolves are very family focused.

As a mother, perfection is just not an option. There is no one way to raise a child and no manual. Each child is vastly different and requires unique tactics, as each child has unique needs. There is a wolf within me that surfaces when my children are attacked or mistreated. A wildness that takes over and my first instinct is to literally tear out the throat of anyone who would harm my offspring, but I feel that this is true for all mothers. We are insatiable in our drive to protect and defend our young.

There isn't a mother (at least, that I have met) that has their "shit together". There are struggles, worries, fears and heartaches that accompany any mother. Sending our children out into the world is a scary thing, especially in the state our world is in now. As a grandmother, watching my own daughter raise her daughter in these times is hard and gut-wrenching as life can be very challenging.

We can learn from the wolves and rally together to protect and defend the young. Regardless of whether they are our children or not, as adults we owe it to future generations to do better for them. What kind of world are we offering them? Do we take care of each other as one universal pack? NO! Something needs to shift on this planet and wolves have the answer. Wolves can teach us how to be better humans if we will only swallow our pride and allow ourselves to be taught.

Give prayers to the Great Mother Wolf, that she may remind humankind where true power lies. It's not in money, status or possessions. Real power and joy of life comes in how we care for others and allow them to care for us. We need to start caring for each other as if we are all mother wolves. Let's invest time, energy, grow and nurture our collective human pack.

CHAPTER SIX

"Isa" Rune of Skadi

Strategy by definition is: "A plan of action designed to achieve a major or overall aim, the art of planning and directing." Skadi is a goddess of strategy. Anyone who lives in the cold must survive by being strategic. Isa is the rune associated with both winter and Skadi. It looks like a capital "I" or a thin, silver blade or shard of ice.

Isa (*ee-saw*) means "ice". This cold element is both beautiful and dangerous. Diana Paxson, a scholar in the runes, writes in her book *Taking up the Runes* that "Ice is hard and without motion. It constrains the movement of the waters, but those who try to walk on it may find themselves moving out of control. Its treachery is passive: it becomes dangerous when humans try to cross it, amplifying their own motions, or emotions, to destroy them."

Ice is hard, sharp, deadly and still. The Isa rune is all about strategy. Whether to act or not to act. To react or not react. To freeze or to thaw. Ice is capable of both, turning water into a solid or melting from solid into flowing brisk liquid. Isa is balanced potential based on one's strategic strength.

"Isa can be the clarity of a cold anger that is so much more dangerous than fiery rage. Its strength is its hardness, but it is brittle, and in working to release a person or a situation from the grip of Isa, one should beware of the energy that will be released when the ice breaks."

When doing rune readings, it is Isa that speaks to me the most. As a passionate person who is quick to react or act when Isa appears, I know that I must freeze, push pause and halt any and all action. This can be very difficult. Over time, Isa has been a rune that I have learned to embrace and appreciate.

Winter is death to those unprepared. Ice is death to those who trample upon it without honoring its silent power. No one but the water knows how strong the ice is until you try to conquer it. We are at the mercy of Nature when it comes to winter and ice. One wrong step and you fall through the ice.

As a silver blade, Isa cuts through the bullshit and gets to the point. After all, a good blade will cut from both sides. This rune is a skillful weapon against ego and arrogance. Winter and ice are humbling. The stillness of winter and the inability to participate and act as one does in the summer months can be overwhelmingly difficult. As humans, we have adopted an instant gratification ideal. As humans, we have arrogantly embraced dominion over the planet and when Mother Nature acts we resist, fight back and we lose every time.

Where I live, we have been known to get intensely cold winters. Living on a dirt road has its challenges but bring on a snow storm and no one to plow our roads and we are homebound, whether we like it or not. This could be terrible if we fought and resisted the process. Instead, we prepare for this because it has happened before and it can always happen again. A nice warm fire, good book and an embracing of the cold that has trapped us inside can be its own kind of welcome magic. It comes down to the strategy that took place before the winter season even begun.

With the first snowfall, I always step outside and sing a song of gratitude to Skadi for tucking us in under her blanket of white. This first snowfall grants permission for things to slow down, for deep internal work to happen and for some stillness from the hustle and bustle of spring, summer and fall. The first snowfall is a welcome sight and a long deep exhale as all that business is released. There is a beautiful calm that arrives.

In Elizabeth Gilbert's book *Eat, Pray, Love* (which became a hit movie featuring Julia Roberts) there is a scene where the main character is in Italy having a discussion in a barber shop wherein one of her new Italian friends introduces her to the concept of "La Dolce Far Niente" which translates as "the sweetness of doing nothing." Let's face it, we are busy bodies; going, going, going … we often do not stop until our head hits the pillow at the end of the day. For some, the idea of not being busy is scary or sounds wasteful, but there is an art to doing nothing and winter gives us time and a reason to attempt this concept of doing nothing. When we allow moments in our day to be guttural or instinctual, without seeking an end result, we enter the present moment and live more consciously.

Can you do that? Can you enjoy the stillness of winter and do nothing? Or will you embrace the noise of television, scrolling on social media platforms or binge-watching a show you have seen before? It's been said that when we embrace the present moment, we allow our true selves to surface because in that stillness of doing nothing we begin to take inventory of our feelings as they are finally allowed to be expressed.

My house is quiet and there is a nice fire going; I could turn on the television and escape reality for a couple of hours before my family returns or I could choose to go outside and look up at the Moon as she rises. What is amazing is that I chose the second option and as I was staring at the Moon, a jet flew over and left a trail behind it in the sky that looked just like the Isa rune. I would have missed this moment if I had chosen to sit and watch television. Unplugging, disconnecting and doing nothing but *being* is the magic – the stillness of being present.

My favorite pastime of doing nothing is sitting outside in the morning, sunbathing and breathing in the new day. Strategy made this possible. We planned and built our porch in just the right spot that it faces the south and is protected from the more than possible north and west winds. Even on a morning where it is 20 degrees, I can sit and just be. Sometimes a good book or warm cup of coffee accompanies me but usually it is just me, the porch and the Sun.

As creatures of checklists and remaining productive, we often feel selfish if we sit and do nothing. I love the quote by Catherine Beard from her blog *The Blissful Mind* where she states that "Life doesn't have to be full to be fulfilling." She goes on to explain her interpretation of La Dolce Far Niente as meaning: "Moments of sweet idleness, we are not forcing anything to happen. We are just responding to what's around us. We are giving our thoughts space to breathe without distraction or expectation."

Have you ever just sat free from distraction and watched the world around you? Or do you find yourself reaching for your phone? What about going on a walk? Do you instantly put on your headphones? I'm sure our ancestors did quite a bit of sitting around a fire in the winter doing nothing but staying warm. I doubt they carried the guilt like we do today in our world of hustle, bustle, to-do lists and feeling like we must be active all day until we drop from exhaustion at the end of the day.

If you have ever gone hiking alone in the winter when there is a blanket of white snow then you know just how quiet the forest becomes. There is stillness so intense that often you do not want to even allow your footsteps to impose. Winter is not everyone's favorite time of year. It is cold; you must be prepared to venture outside and, once out, you are committed to being one with the cold. The desert is my home, sunshine is my friend and heat is my savior. Winter for me can be difficult but with modern conveniences I can tuck myself in and embrace my own kind of hibernation.

The Isa rune is like drawing a line in the sand or snow – a rune of balance, one way and the other. Which side do you choose to stand on? By definition, drawing a line in the sand is all about setting boundaries, "putting a stop to or a limit on something." This act is setting a boundary and making a distinction between what one will allow and what one will no longer tolerate.

When a person stands up and sets a boundary and draws a line in the sand, it doesn't always go over well. There is natural resistance. Holding the line is self-empowerment and can be difficult. When a woman sets a boundary, she is typically referred to as a "bitch, ice queen or prude." When a man sets a boundary, he is typically referred to as a "dick, jerk or a bully." We lack respect for those who stand up for themselves and set healthy boundaries. Of course, the key word is healthy.

There have been many times when I have drawn a line in the sand and stated out loud my boundary. With this act comes accountability and, of course, follow-through. It's hard to say what you mean and mean what you say. With boundaries, the one setting them has to hold them.

Isa reminds me that during the winter I stand on the line, choosing to halt rather than act – to be rather than do. There is a line in a song written by John Lennon that states: "Life is what happens while you're busy making other plans." That to me describes the need to invoke the Isa rune.

We are too busy looking ahead or looking back that we forget to just be consciously here in the present, even if it is for just a few moments, hours, days or, if lucky, a season. How many opportunities have you missed, said no to or been too busy to experience? Yesterday I went to a celebration of life for a friend. At least she was a friend to me, but I was always too busy to make the time and effort or rather to give time and effort. I missed out. As one who lives with not many regrets, I regret being busy and not making time to be conscious in this friendship. I missed out.

While on pilgrimage to England years ago, my lover and I stayed in small towns and we observed something amazing that is not often found in America. Conscious and intentional interaction! In the evenings, the towns came alive as groups, families and friends would pub-hop together, adding people as they went. Each pub was a kaleidoscope of smiling faces, laughter, singing and chatter. Real people disconnecting from the work tasks of the day, not focusing on tomorrow and just being present with each other. Winding down from the day in celebration. It was so inspiring. For me, it was as if the whole town declared "Isa" and time stood still for just a few hours each evening. What a wonderful and welcome sight.

Working with the Isa rune is all about self-inventory, hibernation and seeing when to act and when not too. Think of ice – frozen water that can be transparent, thick and often hard to penetrate. When in hibernation mode, be clear and concise on what you are percolating, be firm and hold steady. Trust yourself and the process of the seasons as they move within you as you.

When we shift our focus and intention to living more consciously connected to Nature as Nature then we begin to feel the seasons stir within us as they stir around us. With winter comes the winding down period, time of rest and reflecting back on the productivity of the year as well as looking forward to the new opportunities. Winter gives us a pause to do just that – to reflect, prepare and be still.

Isa is more a rune of "freezing" rather than taking action. However, it does take great willpower to freeze and not react or act. Think of things in your life that are currently draining you or absorbing all your energy. Can you push pause on these things and go back to them later, after you have recharged? This is freezing. Knowing when to grab the reigns and charge and when not to.

The opposite of freezing is allowing things to thaw. When a river freezes, you see the surface as frozen; you don't see what is happening in the depths. This is true for each individual as one embraces self-inventory. We can freeze what is occurring on the surface but in our depths there may be rapids.

This redirection can be applied to how we view and engage with others. Are we seeing just one's frozen surface and forgetting the depths of their soul? Can we be consciously present when we interact with others and allow them to be? Can we thaw our predisposed judgments? People can change – this is truth – change is the only constant. The more important question is can we *break the ice* and relieve tension with open communication?

When we were in England, enjoying the chatter in the pubs, we did very little talking and more appreciative observation. We saw the energy flowing smooth like a river. There were no icy stares and malicious arguing, just people enjoying each other in the present flow of the evening. There was no need to draw a line and set boundaries, just people being the line, enjoying the balance in being. It was a collective thawing, so to speak.

Isa is many things. Cold, icy and treacherous, yet it can also be stillness – calm and reassuring. After all, winter comes and goes. We don't always have to carry bitterness within, embracing cold-heartedness towards others and situations that we cannot go back to and change. We can thaw hatred, arrogance and break the ice. We can draw a line in the snow/sand and state our boundaries without being ice queens or dicks. We can honor our depths of others that may lie beneath icy stares. Isa is duality. We are Isa. We are winter, spring, summer and fall. We are ice and running waters. We are action and stillness.

Wolves are many things and teach us many things. If you have a dog in your home then you know that they seem to have it easy. At least my dogs do. When I see them lounging on the couch, looking out the window for hours, seemingly content, I often express "oh to be a dog."

Our canine family members appear to have it easy. Their wolf ancestors appeared to live the good life as they sat and basked in the Sun. It all comes down to perspective. Animals are very good at living moment to moment. They do not have the struggles with ego that humans have. Animals are presently content. They know their needs and act on those needs when necessary.

If they have a disagreement then they handle it. If they are hungry then they eat and if they are tired then they sleep. If they are cold, they cuddle up. If they are in need of shelter, they build it. We humans tend to push past our needs, oftentimes unnecessarily. We make our lives difficult.

Wolves are excellent communicators. They don't hold onto grudges and dwell in the past. If conflict happens then it is handled almost as quickly as it began. When every wolf understands that they are a vital participant in the family structure then they naturally work together. There is no time for petty disagreements.

As humans, we waste so much time and energy being offended by every little thing that others do that we forget to live our lives! We become engaged in situations that do not even have anything to do with us and we jump on bandwagons.

Isa is a rune of balance and control. To act or not act. For wolves, Isa too is balance. But for wolves they are all instinct and survival. So if a wolf acts, it is in a need to protect, defend, feed or ensure the safety and survival of the family unit as a whole. For humans, we are very self-motivated and forget that we are part of a much larger family unit.

There are times in life where sometimes pushing pause and sitting in silence can shift the outcome. Have you ever been in an argument and halfway through you forget why you are even upset? Or you forget what you were even fighting about in the first place? What if, instead of investing energy into hair-pulling and defending yourself, you just sat in silence and listened?

EMBRACING THE CALM OF ISA

The next time you find yourself in an argument take a deep breath and freeze your reactions. Picture the rune Isa becoming one with your spine and allow the chill to spread from your spine to your hands, feet and head. Become completely still and quiet your mind. Listen. Just Listen. Silence can speak volumes.

"Silence is true wisdom's best reply."
– Euripides

"Silence is a source of great strength."
– Lao Tzu

"How beautiful it is to stay silent when someone expects you to be enraged."
– Paulo Coelho

"Silence is needed to look and listen inside ourselves for balance, and power to face what goes wrong outside."
– Ingrid Bahtiyar

Uncomfortable conversations, heated arguments and conflicts can quickly become chaos. We become lost in a white-out blizzard situation where things are being said and expressed that are often fueled by ego and emotions. If you have ever found yourself in one of these engagements then you know how quickly they can turn sour. If you have ever found yourself in a white-out snow storm then you know things can become not only sour but deadly very rapidly.

Once, when driving home during a very intense snow storm, I found myself turning down the wrong road, unable to find an outlet to turn around. Panic took hold and I had to do everything in my power to remain calm so that I could safely make it to my home and get out of the storm. Have you ever felt this way during an argument or emotional discussion? This need to get out of it as quickly as possible in order to self-preserve?

White-outs and blizzards can become disorienting. It's easy to become lost. So too can arguments. When emotions are being thrown out from a place of hurt or anger, it's easy to move from active listening to active battling. The "fight or flight" instinct takes hold and everything becomes a mess of chaos that can be hard to pull out of.

Isa can be the answer – the art of pushing pause and still being present in the storm but non-reactive. This is incredibly hard. As a teacher, student and human, I have had situations where disagreements arose and it's so easy to react, to lash out and add to the storm. It is difficult to freeze one's reaction and still be present.

Think of an icicle – it's there in the midst of the blizzard – strong, resilient but not engaged. When it comes to arguments, I do think it's possible to shift from heated argument to productive communication, but there is a time and place. Oftentimes, our first inclination is to react when we feel triggered, jaded or attacked, which causes the other person to react and what should have been a conversation where both parties are encouraged to express and voice their feelings regarding the situation becomes hair pulling.

Conversations that become overpowered by emotions are basically dead in the water. You become lost, disoriented and forget what you were angry about in the first place and both participants step into a way of self-preservation, needing to escape with some sense of dignity.

Recently, I had an argument with my niece and things became heated. A white-out situation occurred and we both escaped the storm with hurt feelings, confusion and frustration. When my sister intervened as peacemaker, she and I had a brief moment where that blizzard and white-out weather began to surface; but rather than let it take over, we both mutually agreed to push pause, to freeze and take a breath together. This freeze changed the direction of the storm and really calmed things down.

We need to get out of this habit in society to demand being heard right in the heat of the moment. There is power when we can push pause, freeze and sit with our feelings for some time. For some, that may mean minutes, hours, days or weeks. Chances are that once you have sat with, honored and allowed your feelings you will lose the need to storm them onto the other party. You will have given yourself time to "*chill out,*" pun intended.

Close your eyes and see yourself standing in the middle of a white-out blizzard, the snow so thick that you couldn't even see your hand if you were holding it in front of your face. Before you allow other emotions to pop, up take a nice slow cleansing breath and freeze. Imagine you are becoming a tall icicle. In this state, the storm can carry on around you but you are held within a layer of protective ice. Take a few deep breaths here and allow the storm to calm around you as you become calmer.

This is an exercise that I have started to implement in my relationships, whether they are casual, work or intimate. Another thing I have started doing is seeing the other person as their own icicle and honoring them for where they are, who they are and seeing them as also needing to protect themselves. This is a simple practice and it really has helped me tremendously.

ACTIVATING THE POWERS OF ICE

Give yourself plenty of time to contemplate and do some self-inventory.

Begin to write down on small post-it papers all the things in your life that you are ready to freeze, disconnect from and no longer engage energetically with.

These can be relationships, work issues, tedious worries, fears etc...

Devote one post-it for each item.

Fold the post-its up, inscribe the Isa rune on each one and place them inside a glass jar.

You may want to express each one out loud as you place them individually in the jar.

Next, pour water over the papers covering them completely.

Seal the jar and inscribe the Isa rune all over the jar,

then place the jar inside a freezer.

This is spell work or focused intention. However you want to define it is completely up to you. The message you are giving the Universe is clear. These are all things that you no longer want to engage with, give your precious time and energy to and so you choose to freeze them. Push pause.

Halt action. Each paper represents a line drawn.

My freezer has quite a few jars tucked in the back. Once placed in the jar, I do not give the issues any more energy. If they pop up from time to time, which does happen, I simply remind myself that I have frozen my interaction with that and move on with my day.

Months, weeks or even years later, when I see that jar in the freezer, I dispose of it by either burying it or allowing it to thaw and then recycling the ingredients and jar and move on. What I have found is that when it comes to relationships in particular, when I disconnect from the tension, freeze my reactions and engagement, the cause of the tension dissipates and I find myself no longer invested.

INVOKING ISA

To invoke means to petition or call upon for assistance, help or support. Many people invoke through prayer, deity work, spell work and conjuring. Anytime we are "casting" there is some kind of call, solicit or appeal being expressed. When working with a rune, you can invoke simply by stating the rune out loud.

When invoking Isa (ee-sah), think of the powers of ice and all that Isa stands for to you. You may be overwhelmed and in need of a reset; what if you go out to your car, sacred space or even your shower and recite Isa out loud?

As an emotional creature I often find myself facing moments where my first instinct is to react, which I know will only make things worse. I have gotten in the habit of stepping outside, taking three deep cleansing breaths and on each exhale voicing out loud: Isa. I do this until I begin to feel calm and the stillness of the Isa rune is activated within me.

You can also inscribe Isa on items such as candles, in your cooking and even on the ground. Literally you can draw that line while invoking Isa. You can also visualize and invoke Isa within you as you. Stand up straight and tall. Think of what you are currently facing that is in need of freezing and visualize your spine lengthening, becoming straight and quite literally becoming the Isa rune from the ground up. State out loud: Isa, over and over again until you feel it in your spine. Feel yourself becoming Isa. Feel yourself become the line of boundaries, the balance within as without. Isa, Isa, Isa.

CHAPTER SEVEN

Goddess of Snow

If you were to walk into a room of 100 individuals and ask them who the Goddess of Winter is you would receive 100 different answers. When it comes to deities, each individual has a unique and distinct insight into and relationship with each unique deity. A google search of "winter goddesses" will pull up just about the same. There is NO one and only Goddess of Winter – there are many! Just as there are many different cultures. Each country, each culture, each pantheon, each religion and each individual has their own Goddess of Winter. Some don't even acknowledge any.

Deity work is personal. There is no right or wrong. While this book is written in devotion to Skadi, it is written through my personal lenses and perspective. When the harvest season begins to wind down, there is a pause, a stand still and limbo stage as winter is just around the corner.

We must have winter, a period of rest to give ourselves, the plants, animals and our Earth (whom some refer to as the Mama or goddess) time. We must go dormant in order to thrive in the coming year. Plants rely upon this period of rest so that they have time to store up energy and prepare for even more growth in the following year.

Our physical bodies need some winter, some time to hibernate. People who are exposed to colder temperatures think clearer and often sleep better. This rest season is vital to our survival.

But winter is vital to the survival of the Earth, which is why she is built in perfect design. Because of the tilt of the Earth's axis, one side must be experiencing winter in order for the other to experience summer. It is the balance of Nature.

While winter is difficult, it is known to be necessary. Honoring a deity and giving them credit for bringing us winter is one way to develop a different perspective, which might make it easier to welcome winter or at the very least give someone to blame.

Quite often, when the first snow begins to fall, I will go outside and sing a song of welcome to Skadi the Goddess of Winter for bringing the snow, for tucking us in under her heavy wet blanket of white. While Skadi is deeply connected with winter, because of her ability to maneuver the landscape with her snowshoes or skis, she is not the only Norse character to be connected to winter sports.

In 1963, the first ever Ullr festival took place at the ski resort in Breckenridge, Colorado. While meant to entice people to embrace the season and take place in winter sports, this festival is filled with misinformation and the glorifying of someone who is not a god or ever known to be a god.

In Norse mythology, there is no known God of Skiing. This is a good time to reiterate that Skadi was not officially a goddess; she was a Giantess who was embraced as one of the gods when she married the Sea God Njord. She was however referred to as "Ski Goddess."

Ullr festivals are marketing events. The ones that I have personally witnessed are nothing but a mockery of the old ways and depict the Norse deities as nothing more than Hagar the Horrible from the comic strip that came out in the 70's. There is no prayer to the actual bringer of snow. Most of these festivals consist of someone dressed up very poorly in a Halloween costume that is supposed to represent a god. This impersonator then races down the mountain on skis and then lights the skis on fire. There is of course mass drinking and the entire charade is supposed to please the gods that they will bless the ski resort with an abundance of snow so that financially they will survive. Clearly I am not a fan or in support of these festivals. Some could say that I take my relationship with the Old One's very seriously and would rather not associate or support an establishment that mocks them.

With that said, things are shifting and more people are starting to realize that Ullr is not a god, he does not bring the snow and he is really only mentioned briefly and that is to describe him wearing skis. Stepson of Thor, son of Sif, he is said to be the cause of the Northern Lights being formed by his speed in skiing through the skies. For those things we can offer him credit.

Skadi is being called upon by some ski resorts and she is being given credit and praise for bringing the snow. This is a much more fitting shift and rather less of a mockery in my humble opinion.

Skadi is credited for teaching people how to ski, which also makes more sense.

Skadi's home in the northern province of Northern Norway, along with her characteristics and attributes has connected her to the Sami indigenous people of Finland, Sweden, Norway and Russia. Hilda Ellis Davidson, a scholar, proposes that Skadi had indeed a cult following. As she was one of the Jötuns (a prehistoric race that predated the Vanir and Aesir), it is impossible to calculate how old Skadi was. In the Scandinavian Peninsula there were two groups the Sami and Nordic peoples. It is possible that Skadi influenced the Saami people and vice versa.

One speculated *"oldest set of skis"* was found near Lake Sindor in Russia and dated back to 6300 BC. The Sami honor skis as a method of transportation and they credit their ancestors with inventing them. The word ski in Old Norse means "split piece of firewood." There have been rock drawings depicting a man on skis holding onto a stick found on the Norwegian islands as well as in Norway. Skiing is said to be one of the oldest sports in existence. Another pair of skis was found in Kalvstrassk, Sweden, carbon-dated to about 5200 years old.

Still, the burning of skis bothers me. Skis were a very essential form of transportation and quite literally would ensure the survival of the individual; I honestly doubt that they would burn something so sacred. But, what do I know? With most early Pagan traditions being oral in preservation, one can never have absolute truth as to what really happened, let alone what was really sacrificed.

With the rise of Modern Age pagan practices, more and more people are starting to speak out and question festivals such as the Ullr ones and things are shifting. Most ski resorts (for environmental reasons) no longer burn skis and instead focus on pouring out libations and offerings to the gods of winter with ale, mead and plenty of communal feasting.

Ritual sacrifices or "blot" sacrifices ensured honor to the gods. These sacrifices were an exchange and offering. Many animals were offered to the gods in exchange for their blessing upon the land, crops and community. Pouring out a horn filled with mead upon the ground or altar stone is a form of sacrifice and offering made to one particular god or goddess. Along with mead; ale, animals, jewelry, tools, blood and humans were all discovered to be utilized at major sacrificial sacred sites. So the sacrificing of skis and snowshoes is a possibility. It has been argued however that the burning of these items would not be a welcome sacrifice to the gods as they would be considered damaged.

What's also funny to me is when Ullr is referred to as a "Patron Saint!" This terminology is such a contradiction when attached to a Pagan. While some resorts and communities honor both Skadi and Ullr together in the winter season, it is done out of tribute to both. For me, Ullr was embraced in America because skiing was a predominantly male sport so, naturally, having a male as their god of the season worked for many. But many are outgrowing the ruling of the patriarch.

It is rumored that Skadi is married to Ullr but there is no concrete proof, only speculation. For me, I prefer to see Skadi as the one who brings the snow and the one who teaches us how to survive through the hardships of winter. Skadi is fierce, strategic and knows the mountains. With her bow, arrows, snowshoes and animal hide she shows us that living in the winter takes fierce courage, strategy and a very in-depth understanding of the mountains and weather.

As one who does not ski or engage in winter sports (even though I live 40 minutes from a major ski resort), I still know there are some things that are basic understanding when it comes to winter. One needs to be prepared and have basic knowledge in order to survive. We are spoiled with our electricity, central heating and modern homes. Our ancestors were not! They relied heavily on their preparation in the summer/fall in order to hope to survive the winter (emphasis on hope).

Approaching the winter could be compared to approaching a wolf pack. There needs to be some knowledge, strategy and deep respect. Nature in all her forms; weather or animal, are to be honored and respected, for we are the intruders. When it comes to the elements, we are at the mercy of those who control it.

Winter is not something to take lightly, unless one simply doesn't value life. Winter was and is for many a very dark time of the year. For the ancestors, there was feasting and bonfires to create merriment amongst the clans and tribes. These events created hope, just as seeing the Sun stay out longer each day was also a beacon of hope.

Recently I attended a class on another winter goddess – the Cailleach, an Irish goddess who begins her seasonal reign around the end of the harvest season in late October to early November. She is a weather hag who brings about that first biting chill in the air – that seasonal shift when your breath begins to show and air becomes fierce with frost. This "bite" is the breath of the Cailleach!

Known throughout Scotland, England and Ireland, this old hag, depicted as wearing a long cloak that covers most of her face, is ancient, withered and weathered with age. She is complex, both dark and light in her aspects. She is the keeper of many animals such as deer, wild cattle, goats and cats, but she is also the watcher of wolves. Sound familiar?

Cailleach in Gaelic means "veiled one". Because the Celtic tradition (similar to the Norse) is primarily oral, there is no actual written document that states whether the Cailleach is mythical or a real person, but she is a force that is both feared, respected and honored.

Imbolc (*em-olc*) is a seasonal shift that is celebrated around February 1st. This celebration marks the quickening of spring and the flow of milk. Legend has it that the Cailleach is running low on her winter supply at this time so, if the day is sunny, she will be out gathering more wood to ensure that she has enough for the next six weeks. If the day is wet and stormy, she will bring about an early spring. This tradition has been widely accepted in the United States – we call it Groundhog Day.

The Cailleach is connected to the Patron Saint of Ireland, the Goddess Brigid, for Brigid is the ruler of the summer months, being given this role from the Cailleach who hands Brigid her reign on May 1st, at which time the Cailleach turns into a stone until her return to reign at the end of October.

The Cailleach is the force that shapes the landscape. There are many standing stones, mountains and landmarks dedicated to her. She is associated with more sacred sites in the "Gaelic-speaking" world than any other deity in Scotland or Ireland.

As a deity of the land, she is often referred to as "*mother*" of the gods and goddesses in Scotland. Despite her being connected to so many sacred landmarks, she is often overlooked. She is ancient and predates Celtic mythology. Her many names include and are not limited to the Blue Hag of Winter, Old One, witch, Bone Mother, Woman of Stones, Cailleach Bheur, Beira, Cally Berry, The Great Old Woman of the Deer, Old Woman of the Speckled Mountains and Goddess of Destruction.

As a weather witch (referred to as Bheur, which means "sharp"), she is the one who brings the cold, wintry storms of snow and frost. The class that I attended was near the Full Moon of February, this is known as the Snow Moon. Winter is often connected to wolves, as they do not hibernate. Their thick hide of fur allows them to hunt and remain active during this time of the year, which is why the Cailleach and Skadi are both associated with wolves.

Both of these goddesses of winter are portrayed as dark and light, their messages similar yet distinct. The Cailleach is one that is often feared, as you can hear her cackle of control as she sends the bitter snowfall that traps one indoors, while Skadi emits a laughter of bliss as she gifts the snow for us to enjoy and engage in – not be bound by.

Cailleach and Skadi are both role-models for strategy and planning ahead, making the most of the season both out of necessity and pleasure. The Cailleach can be frightening as she brings the reality of winter, being connected with death. One must respect the cold or die from it. Skadi is strength, overcoming that fear of death and ensuring one's survival while enjoying the change in season.

When it comes to embracing any seasonal deity, you should really take inventory of your personal relationship with the seasons. Ask yourself how a deity is going to help you make the most of the season that you are wanting to embrace. For me, winter is both light and dark. The stillness that comes is calming and gives me an opportunity to heal. However, the storms can be so intense and frightening that fear can surface rapidly. Finding a balance is key. Working with both the Cailleach and Skadi can help.

Often I am asked: "Who do you worship?" I find that this question surfaces quite a bit when mentioning any of the gods or goddesses. My reply is always: "No one." When it comes to deity work, that is a very personal relationship and there is no cut-and-dried, this way is the right way. It's an individual relationship.

Deities for me are mirrors. They show me attributes which I already possess. In the winter months, I can fear the winter that the Cailleach brings or I can welcome it. Within me there is an icy chill that can frighten others and it is up to me to create that storm or calm it. Also within me there is a forceful strength that can be intimidating or repelling.

As mirrors, the Cailleach and Skadi show me that when I meditate or call to them, they remind me what I am capable of and what I can do more of to ensure that myself and my family survive the winter, whether it is a physical winter or an energetic one.

Animals are mirrors and oftentimes people can relate more to an animal than a deity from the past. My entire life has been blessed with animals, both in the home and out. Animals have always fascinated and inspired me. When you look to animals as the gods, things shift in many ways – from what you eat, to the way you shop and live.

There are animals that thrive in winter climates! They literally show us the way to enhance our own personal experiences with the cold. Some animals hibernate, mirroring to us the need for rest. Just as Skadi and the Cailleach have much to offer us, mirror to us and teach us, so to do the animals.

Many look to animals as gods, not out of worship, but respect! When I call upon an animal as guide it is to remind me that I too am part beast and I too can not only survive but I can thrive despite the hardships I may be facing.

There are many animals that are considered gods of winter, all of which have their own unique strengths. Just like Skadi and the Cailleach, they show us a different way to welcome the cold. For example, polar bears, harp seals, gentoo penguins, caribou, wood frogs, squirrels, beavers, black-capped chickadees, white-tailed deer, snowy owls, snow leopards, walruses, beluga whales and, of course, the family of Arctic beasts – fox, hare and wolf.

As one who has spent the better part of this past decade in devotion to wolves as teacher, for me the Arctic wolves are to be considered and seen as gods of winter. Arctic wolves are smaller than their subspecies relative, the grey wolf. Both the Arctic wolf and timber wolf are the only wolves that can still be found in their original habitat, this is mostly due to the decrease in the number of humans interfering.

These majestic creatures measure about three to six feet from nose to end of tail. They weigh in at just under 200 pounds. They will roam up to 1000 square miles, hunting migrating caribou and musk ox.

Each individual wolf is part of a greater whole. In the book *Among Wolves*, written by scientist Gordon Haber, he says that: "Wolves are not just individual animals, but a highly social, efficiently coordinated group where each wolf knows its position. All wolves are involved in the day-to-day survival of the entire family from the building of dens and raising of pups, to the hunt. Each wolf plays a role that is irreplaceable; making each wolf vital and necessary.

With Arctic wolves (also known as polar wolves or white wolves), their fur is typically white, which allows them to be camouflaged against the snow, but they can also be grey, black or tan. To protect themselves from the elements, they have a thick layer of body fat which is added insulation and their paws are covered with fur.

For centuries, wolves have been worshipped, revered and considered divine messengers and gods that walk amongst us. From Rome, Japan, Egypt, Italy to the Inuits, Norse, Celts, Native Americans and Chinse – wolves are honored and respected.

The Inuit people are indigenous inhabitants of the Arctic and Subarctic regions of Greenland, Canada and Alaska. Their religion mainly consisted of animism and shamanism, although today many follow Christian theologies. Their beliefs, similar to the Norse and Celts, are primarily oral myths, legends and traditions, passed down from generation to generation with very little if any written forms.

Amarok or Amaguq is the gigantic Wolf God who stalks, kills and devours any person who is careless enough to hunt alone at night. Unlike wolves that hunt in a pack or family group, Amarok hunts alone. Some believe that this enormous wolf creature originated from the ancient Eskimo's stories of the dire wolf.

My favorite story of Amarok is when a boy in the nearby village that suffers from deformities and is teased and taunted cries out to Amarok (also known as "Lord of Strength") to assist him in overcoming his weaknesses. Amarok appears and demands that the boy wrestles him, during which many of the bones in the boy's body are broken. Amarok tells the boy that the breaking is all part of the process and that the bones which shattered were holding him back and preventing him from being strong and healed. Amarok demands that the boy comes back and fights him for several days in order to overcome and develop his strength. At the end of his days fighting the great wolf Amarok, the boy is so strong that when three large bears attack his village; he fights them off – thus winning the respect of his village.

What does Amarok mirror to us? Well, for one, Amarok encourages wit and strategy. It's not smart to go hunting alone in the night! Amarok also mirrors to us perseverance and determination, much like Skadi. Like the Cailleach, sometimes the path ahead may look frightening and you may lack confidence and apprehension in moving forward, yet great strength awaits those who push onward despite the fear.

MEDITATING WITH THE GODDESS OF WINTER

Allow your eyelids to simply rest and bring your focus to your breath. Take a nice, slow and conscious inhale, followed by a healing, cleansing exhale. Repeat this for up to five breath cycles. While you breathe, allow all the muscles within your physical body to relax.

Give yourself permission to also allow your mind to relax. When a wandering thought surfaces, simply exhale it away.

Now take your breath a bit deeper by inhaling to the count of four and .exhaling to the count of four. Repeat this for about six to nine times.

Once you feel your body letting go physically, you are ready to move a bit deeper.

In this state, activate your mind's eye. Focus on visualization and see yourself standing in the middle of a forest. Breathe in this forest. See the tall evergreens and see how thick and dense they are. On the ground beneath you is snow – a thick blanket of white.

You stand supported by your snowshoes atop the snow.

With each breath you exhale, you see the proof of just how cold it really is. But you are warm, protected by the layers of fur that you are wearing. In the distance you hear the howling of wolves and above through the trees you see the sky is clear and the stars are shining brightly.

There is a quiet and stillness that can feel unnerving but you remain where you stand, unwilling to disturb the peace with the crunch of snowshoes on the snow. So here you stand in the midst of winter. How does it feel? What is winter to you?

You may find that you are now sitting upon the snow, somewhat held and comforted by the silence, despite how eerie it may be at times. There is healing when one can quiet one's inner storm and a chill that takes over as the frost settles.

(Pause)

Here in the forest of your mind, a choice is necessary, for one cannot sit upon the snow forever. So you stand up and take a few steps, moving into the trees. You observe two pathways. One is dark, stormy and unpredictable; the other steep, slick and rocky.

Which one will you choose?

As you stand here, you see two figures approaching you. One is veiled with a thick heavy hood that covers from head to foot; you see only a glimpse of blue-tinged icy fingers holding a staff. The other is tall, scratches on her face; she is wearing fur, leather and has a bow and arrow.

One of them beckons you to follow them.

The Cailleach will lead you into the brisk, icy, unknown storm. Skadi will challenge you to climb up the slick rocky surface to the top of the mountain. The choice is yours and only you need know why you pick the path you choose.

With your pathway chosen, you begin your journey. You do not walk alone. No one walks before you, clearing the path of debris; instead they simply walk beside you.

Meditation Response:

In life, we are always given options. Some of us dive into the depths of choppy waters, while others choose the calm streams. In this case, you were given two unpleasant options to choose from. Winter is not for the faint-of-heart. It is not gentle; there is always a give and take. If you chose the pathway of the Cailleach then you are ready to enter the unknown, at the same time knowing it will not always be easy. If you chose the pathway of Skadi then you know you must activate strength to reach the top. Both paths are challenges, both deities are guides and it's up to you to make it through the dark or make it to the top.

CHAPTER EIGHT

Harnessing the Cold

The cold, brisk, icy chill of winter can be felt physically and energetically. We are creatures that live on an unpredictable planet. We are at the mercy of Nature when it comes to the weather. Winter is no picnic! Winter can decrease feel-good hormones, tighten airways, increase blood pressure and wreak havoc on even the most healthy. There has to be a period of adapting, which is vital to survival.

How can we strengthen our bodies and minds? How can we harness the cold to both physically and energetically power us? Skadi as Frost Giantess was made from the elements and was therefore one with the elements. We naturally anchor into our environments. We become adapted. As one who lives in the desert, I find a power and energy source from being outside in the dry heat all day, while others may find themselves being weakened.

When it comes to harnessing the cold and working with it through strategic physical and mental strength increases, we can become emboldened and invigorated. To test this theory and implement this concept I picked up the book *The Wim Hoff Method* by Wim Hoff, who is known as the "Iceman".

People who challenge their bodies physically and mentally are inspirational. As one who was somewhat familiar with Wim Hoff and his method, reading his book and implementing this method into my life over the past several months has been enlightening.

His approach is simple but when actually implemented, it is a challenge, which is something that I find completely enticing. He states in the first few pages that: "You must immerse yourself in Nature, in the elements, so much that your body is working in its depth and all the senses of your being are truly activated – then the mind and Nature are one." He goes on to empower with his words saying: "There is so much more to life than meets the eye, if you choose to seek it. The seeker becomes the finder; the finder of so much more than we thought was possible. We are beings of light who, by birthright, own our own minds and souls. This is the time to wake up to the true power we each possess within us. We have nothing to combat but our own conditioning and fear."

Going from desert heat to embracing cold was not going to be easy. If I was going to understand the mental and physical strength that Skadi had then I needed to test my body and challenge it. I needed to get out of my comfort zone and move away from what my body was conditioned to handle. To do this, I started with Wim Hoff's challenge of a cold shower every day. While this may not seem like a big thing, I dare you to try it. When I shower, like most women, the water temperature has to be near scalding! So going from heat to cold was quite literally shocking!

Cold showers are incredibly good for you! They increase circulation, reduce muscle soreness, stimulate the vascular system, increase energy, increase stamina, stimulate metabolism and strengthen one's willpower. The first time I took a cold shower I really had to breathe through it. Every part of my body was screaming! Now, after several months, my hot part of the shower has drastically been decreased and I look forward to ending with the cold.

When we went on vacation in Hawaii, I found myself experiencing some heat exhaustion after a very long day playing in the Sun. I began to have a headache, feel slightly nauseous and my skin was quite sunburned. My solution and savior was a two and a half minute cold shower. Wim Hoff describes how: "Cold leads the way toward a spirituality of the mind, a calmness with which you can handle any other stress."

When we create physical discomfort, such as going from a hot pleasant and relaxing shower to a biting cold, freezing stream of water cascading upon us, we create stress that our bodies and minds have to react to. If you tense up and breathe rapidly you resist the process and can create harm within your body. If you focus on your breath, slowing your heart rate down, you create power! Mind power!!! Truly, if you think it – you create it. When it comes to embracing the cold, it is all about dedication and your individual mindset.

Skadi was a determined and confident warrior. She was skilled in fighting. Was she born this way? NO! As with any physical skill, in order to be good at it, one must work hard, train hard and test one's strength in order to find the weaknesses and make them stronger. Any athlete will tell you that they worked incredibly hard, stressed their bodies, healed their bodies and fueled their bodies to mold them and shape them into conquerors.

Skadi not only teaches us that one can survive in the cold but one can also enjoy it! She tells us to get out in the cold weather and make the most of it! Now, again, I am not a skier! Nor have I ever snowshoed. But I have learned to enjoy things like shoveling snow. Disliking the winter, the snow and the cold was an obstacle that needed to be worked through if I was going to enhance and welcome a working relationship with Skadi.

I started with something small like smiling while shoveling the walkway or taking cold showers (a meditative experience), which were both small acts that have greatly increased my mental and physical wellbeing. Any time we engage in things that are outside of our comfort zone, we become more in control of our reactions and emotions. We become better equipped to handle the stresses within our lives.

Just 30 seconds of a cold shower every day can reduce inflammation, soreness and improve the function of one's immune system. Cold showers at least three times a week for six weeks greatly increase the number of lymphocytes – a type of white blood cell that combats bacteria, toxins and viruses. Cold therapy benefits immunity. Cold exposure increases mental toughness!

What I have observed within my own body is an increase in energy and confidence. My sleep quality has improved and bouts of anxiety are lessened. When a headache comes on, anxiety begins or a sore throat or physical dis-ease creeps in, I head into the cold shower. Mind over matter! Wim Hoff, like so many, is extraordinary! He firmly believes that: "We are limited only by the depth of our imagination and our strength of conviction."

Fear is a heavy weight that drags us down into our depths and forces us to either sink or rise above. It is hard to combat fear. I'm sure Skadi had some fear when she marched into the great hall, demanding justice for her father's death. Yet she persevered.

The cold of winter can bring a similar heaviness with it. Especially for those who experience seasonal depression and winter fatigue. Cold weather can create havoc. Winter can trigger asthma, allergies, raise blood-pressure, raise blood-sugar levels and cause stiffness in joints for those who have arthritis.

Winter blues or winter depression can start to show up with that first biting chill. For most with this dis-ease, they feel sluggish, heavy, and experience a loss of interest in activities that they usually enjoy. They can become sad, hopeless, crave comfort foods and have difficulty concentrating. Most of this is due to the fact that the cold of winter keeps us indoors, away from the Sun. We have within us a biological clock or circadian rhythm. When there is a decrease in sunlight, our internal clock is disrupted. Our serotonin levels drop along with our body's level of melatonin.

These are very real physical disruptions and can be detrimental. While there are many ways to approach these blues, healing and understanding one's own unique body chemistry and emotional needs are top priority. When it comes to making the most of winter and harnessing the power of cold, this could be quite difficult for those who dread the cold because of the heaviness of seasonal woes that can accompany it.

How can you shift perspective? How can you push past this physical barrier and really enhance your seasonal experiences? How can you harness the strength of Skadi and learn to love the shift in seasons?

Our bodies crave balance between hot/cold, light/dark, day/night – we need this balance amongst the polarities. With winter, we need to create heat, not just physically but internally. We need to get our bodies and souls warm from the inside out. There are many ways to activate heat, even in the crisp freeze of winter.

Activate by moving. Our bodies are not designed to be stagnant. Even though our natural inclination when the weather turns is to burrow under blankets beside a warm fire and sip hot cocoa, our bodies need movement. When the cold creeps in, we can feel it in our joints – this is what becomes painful for those who have arthritis or have had surgeries and have metal inside them. We need to stretch, bend and exercise! Yoga for the joints and high interval cardio training for circulation.

There are three steps in the Wim Hoff method – the first being cold immersion, the second is breath and the third is mindset. When we breathe deeply and activate our breath, we focus on "filling the belly and letting it go, like a wave. Breathing fully in, letting go, fully in, letting go. Find your rhythm and follow it." The Wim Hoff breathing method pushes carbon dioxide out of your body and replaces it with oxygen. This creates more alkalinity within.

Combining yoga with Wim Hoff breathing has really helped me increase flexibility and maintain control over my emotional ups and downs – activating both my mind and my body to create

SKADI

heat within my entire physical body and this warms me up with confidence.

Bring the power of the Sun inside. Vitamin D is good for us! Sunshine really boosts that happy hormone serotonin. In the winter it can be hard to go outside and sit in the Sun, but when we open the windows, we let the Sun shine in. There are light therapy lamps that you can purchase and place in your home to effectively ward off seasonal winter blues.

Awaken your creative side. During the winter months (when you may feel trapped indoors) is the perfect time to take up a creative craft, start an indoor remodel project or take up knitting. Activate your mind by challenging it to learn something new or create something new. If you already are an artist, why not dedicate each winter to using a new medium? The winter gives me plenty of indoor time where I can write. What is something you have always wanted to do artistically? Why not take the winter and give it a shot?

Stimulate your mind. We live in a world where technology has given us hands-on access with the push of a button to just about everything. Why not embrace the winter and enroll in an online class?

There is a natural excitement and internal challenge that happens when we venture out of our comfort zone and learn something new. Online classes are super-easy ways to stay indoors and keep warm but still stimulate your brain, which will warm you up in a totally different way.

Take up baking. Winter is filled with plenty of seasonal goodies and treats. Why not be experimental and warm up your kitchen at the same time? Give yourself the challenge of baking something new every couple days just to spice things up.

Read a book or two or three! Our ancestors didn't have television like we do today. They didn't have the internet. They

102

told stories, they sang songs around the fire. They entertained each other. We as a society have become complacent, there is only so much TV one can watch before they start to become depressed about wasting a whole day binge-watching. The goal in embracing the cold is to avoid becoming depressed. So, maybe turn the TV off and pick up a book. Read a book out loud as a family. Write down your family stories and create a book! As an avid reader, nothing warms me up more than escaping into a whole new world created on the pages of a good book.

Play in the snow! Skadi lived alone on her mountain with her wolves. She didn't hide away or count down the days until winter ended. She was outside in the cold! Put on those skis or snowshoes, bundle up and breathe in some cold winter air and be amongst the elements. Winter seems long but so does summer. We need to embrace the time we have to be consciously present in each.

Learn to adapt! By definition, adaptability means: "The quality of being able to adjust to new conditions." As humans, we are capable of adapting. We have simply become complacent in our comforts. When we are forced to move outside of our realm of this complacency, we resist and that which we resist seems to persist; at least, until we have learned our lesson.

Inspiration comes from many different people, places and experiences. There is a slogan by the Marines that really stands out: "Adapt, Improvise, Overcome." This is a mindset! This way of thinking can help individuals to overcome any obstacle, whether that is mental, physical or spiritual. How often do we rise above and keep moving forward, despite the challenge we are currently facing?

Winter is a season that is unpredictable! For example, as I write this, it is February and the weather outside is 24 degrees with about ten inches of snow. January was very warm, with no snow and the temperatures reached about 56 degrees. This is unusual but completely out of one's control. Time to adapt! This morning, instead of sitting outside and drinking my coffee soaking up the sunrise, I went out in snow boots and shoveled snow. Life is unpredictable. When we invest energy into controlling every detail, we miss the point of living consciously.

Anytime a new book is birthed, there are ample amounts of research that come with it. Today, while shoveling snow, I was implementing research and shifting my perspective. Also, I was watching my son's dog who refused to come inside; to the point that, when I went towards the door, he laid down on the ground on his belly as if he was clutching the ground in protest of having to go inside. He was teaching me to play and be present, so I stayed outside for a bit longer. He was teaching me to embrace and find the fun, rather than dwell on the fact that it was cold.

Undisturbed snow is my favorite. It sparkles. Looking at the ample amount of snow reassured me that this spring will come abundance, as the plants beneath it were being given a chance to percolate a bit more. Snow is vital. It's not always convenient but it is necessary.

There are times in our lives where we choose to hold winter in our hearts. Cold-hearted tendencies reflect disapproval, lack of sympathy, detachment, indifference and harsh treatment. This is the Ice Queen archetype in action. Just like the seasons, we can learn to allow this coldness within to surface periodically, rather than daily. There is a time and purpose for all things.

When it comes to harnessing the power of the cold, this can be applied to both the weather and to our internal emotions. Start with inventory. Why have you chosen to become distant? What purpose will it serve to freeze up and be chilly towards others? Once the outcome you desired has been achieved, how can you defrost? Do you even want to defrost? Do you want to create warmth within?

There are many times in life where freezing emotional attachments is vital to our survival. But there are also times where staying in that state of chill can become a blockage to progress. To find the balance is to be adaptable. It is possible – difficult but possible.

Wim Hoff offers this insight: "Let go of your ego and instead reflect that which connects us, which is love. Let go of your thoughts and your stress and open up to your heart. It is only when you let go that you will truly be able to reconnect with the Universe, with the Nature buried deep within your cells. Let go and allow your soul to rise in your consciousness. The soul is eternal, indestructible and, perhaps most importantly, incorruptible."

Harness the power of being one with Nature. Ride out the seasonal shifts with gratitude and appreciation, for each season offers us opportunities to grow and expand. Harness the power of Nature within your body, for you are nature. Ride out those emotional shifts, let them be expressed, felt and allowed (within reason) and welcome the expansion. There is power in the calm of winter and it mirrors to us our own power, our own capabilities to adapt and grow. We are powerful and we can create external warmth and internal warmth. Life is a process of living actively conscious.

Winter, like any of the seasons, has its own strengths, its own power, its highs and lows and when embraced it can offer us strength and power. Fear is the culprit that prevents us from moving forward. As long as you are prepared and have what you need to protect you from the elements, you can enjoy and make the most of the elements.

Wolves are excellent at adapting to drastic changes in weather. Wolves are the greatest teachers to humans, if we would only allow ourselves to be taught by them. When winter begins, wolves' fur begins to thicken providing them with insulation. They dig their dens a little deeper and they know that the best way to stay warm is by keeping their paws and noses warm.

While we lack fur, we do not lack options of insulated clothing. The best trick to keeping your body warm and safe in wet cold temperatures is to keep feet, hands and face warm and dry. Wolves teach us to adapt – to prepare our dens and to know when to cuddle up and when to run and hunt.

Most will agree that the hardship of winter comes in the form of isolation and solitude. In the winter, most of us are not out at the lake, camping with friends or attending large gatherings. It's cold! Snow conditions make roads difficult for commutes and if depression sinks in seasonally then leaving the house is not always an emotional option.

Aristotle said: "Whosoever is delighted in solitude is either a wild beast or a god." Skadi to me is both wild beast and god. She appears to enjoy her solitude on her mountain. But is she really alone? Wolves, just like our furry friends in our homes, provide excellent and somewhat preferred companionship. Maybe we connect Skadi to solitude because she is selective in who she spends her time with. Is this really a bad trait?

As a dog owner, I can safely say that I often prefer the company of my dogs to people. My dogs don't judge me when I have an emotional day and need a good cry. There is a safety and security in animal companionship, which is why many people own emotional support animals. Animals can and do give us unconditional love. They know how to comfort, and when.

Skadi shows us that we are capable of surviving hard things. We are stronger than the limitations we give ourselves and we can survive the physical and emotional chills in our life with a bit of physical preparation, adaptation and a positive mindset. Our perspective is power or downfall.

Again, wolves show us that we are stronger when we band together; when we have a family unit, tribe, clan or pack to support us and cheer us on. Encouragement goes a long way! Even when we sink into those depths where we freeze contact out of self-preservation, we need to know that there are friends who are not taking it personally, who are there when we need them and who are not offended when we move deep into our dens to do some self-inventory.

Who do you have in your life that helps you weather your personal storms? Are you that person for others? Showing up for others is not always easy or convenient but there's going to be many times where as individuals we are going to need someone to show up for us. You get what you give in life and that applies to the investment, time and energy you offer to the people in your life.

Winter comes and goes, people come and go. Through our interactions we learn who is here to stay. Family can be a constant for some and for others a terrible nightmare. The families we make along the way seem to create impacting relationships. These relationships are the ones that matter; they feed us and keep us energetically warm, they provide us with strength and encouragement. Everyone wants someone in their corner, someone who has their back, someone they can call when life gets icy.

This need for companionship applies to intimate, romantic unions as well. We have a basic human need for affection and love. We have one very basic need, and that is for survival. A long cold winter can mean life or death, depending on the planning and prepping that took place in the summer months. The same goes for our relationships. We can fuel them by providing warmth for each other or we can create an icy chill that will freeze and harden our hearts. Skadi mirrors to us the capability to strategically select who is in our pack and who can be our mate. She offers us strength of individual choice!

CHAPTER NINE

Njord and Skadi
Sacred Union

There is chaos, laughter, talking, drinking and feasting inside the great hall. One can easily feel the merriment from outside. With an anger boiling up in rage and vengeance, Skadi the Giantess, armed with bow and arrows, her snowshoes strapped to her back and sword in hand, has nothing but ferocious blood thirst as she thrusts open the doors of Odin's hall. She commands silence with her combative entrance.

Odin, the Allfather, not being one to invest much time in bloodshed while a feast is going on, quickly goes into action. He gives the Skadi his full respect and allows her the floor to demand justice for her father's death. She demands the death of Loki. Odin is wise and has his own blood oath with Loki, so he makes a wager. What if he gives her a husband of her choosing from the gods who sit amongst them in the hall? This act would after all make her an equal and one with the gods. She accepts this offer but Odin adds a twist. Skadi could have her pick of the gods to marry but she must make her selection based solely on the appearance of the prospective husbands' feet.

The gods line up behind a curtain and expose only their bare feet. Skadi looks over the feet, one by one, examining them thoroughly, while in her mind she longs to find the feet belonging to Baldur, the shining bright, golden son of Odin and Frigga. Baldur, Skadi thought, must have the most beautiful looking pair of feet. She makes her decision based on this ideal and to her disappointment she finds that the most beautiful pair of feet actually belongs to Njord, the God of the Sea.

Oaths and agreements are not only honored, they are binding. Skadi agreed to this wager and she married Njord. She was now an equal amongst the gods, as she was now one of them. Njord too, agreed to this wager and he went through with the marriage. This much we know, as this nuptial story is very much a main part of the brief mention of Skadi the Giantess.

The two were married. Because they were both rulers of their own realms, they decided to split time amongst the realm of the sea and the mountaintop. For nine days and nine nights, Skadi slept on Njord's ship upon the crashing waves and she was awakened by the screeching of seagulls – she was miserable. She longed for the quiet peace of the mountain and the warmth and companionship of her wolves.

In return, Njord spent nine days and nine nights on top of the mountain in the bitter stillness of the freezing temperatures and he was kept awake at night by the howling of wolves – he was miserable.

So they made a new agreement. They would end their marriage due to mutual dislike of each other's realms. This was done in a very mature fashion and both remained friends. It is said that Skadi also spent some time with Odin in a wifely state and bore him many sons.

Marriage is a compromise in many ways. Taking two very unique individuals and having them share the same living space offers plenty of learning curves. There is much to learn from the brief union of Skadi and Njord, which is why I believe their story is mentioned in the first place.

Marriage amongst the early Pagans of Scandinavia was a contract, often a business-type arrangement between families.

There was an exchange of silver, given as a bride price or dowry. This was typically not forced but an agreement made between the bride, groom and their families. Marriages were often out of a need to unite or form an alliance between families or as a way of ending feuds. Mostly, they were political or the families gained some kind of economic status. Again, neither party was forced. Marriage was a serious strategic contract.

These unions were ahead of the time, as far as women rights were concerned. Women could refuse the offer of marriage and if the marriage wasn't to their liking then they could initiate divorce. This was pretty much unheard of in other regions, cultures and pantheons. In other parts of Europe and really the world in general, a woman being able to end the marriage was simply not allowed!

Women could seek divorce for practically any reason and could remarry as many times as they wanted. "Despite the Viking Age being viewed as male-centric, Norse women enjoyed certain rights and freedoms that were vastly ahead of their time."

There is a distinct difference between what we today refer to as a marriage and what the early agricultural people defined a union between two people as being. Many modern-day wedding traditions predate Christianity. When discussing the union between Skadi and Njord, it is vital to acknowledge a difference in beliefs and customs.

Modern paganism, which is the recreation of the indigenous spiritual traditions of Europe, is the fastest growing practice in the world today. More and more people are turning to paganism as a way to define their religious views and as a way to live their lives.

There is a resurgence of handfasting ceremonies wherein couples are bound at the wrists and swear oaths and make commitments to each other. This binding of the hands is where the terminology "tying the knot" comes from. Typically, this union lasts for a year and a day but most of these ceremonies that take place today are done in place of the traditional wedding ceremony, so there is not a time-frame on it unless specified by the couple.

As a minister it has been my honor to handfast numerous couples in the tradition of modern paganism. Some weddings have been more Celtic, Norse and Wiccan in design but ultimately each of these unions caters to the individuals choosing to be with each other, live with each other, care for each other and love each other. Handfastings are not sanctioned by a Christian God nor do they require a legal religious officiate. A couple can choose to handfast without anyone present, as it is their commitments and vows to each other that really matter. A couple can also choose to legitimize their union by filing the legal paperwork and having the handfasting performed by a licensed minister.

It has only been in the past 200 years or so that nations have passed legislation requiring couples to be legally married. Njord and Skadi most likely engaged in a handfasting ceremony where they made the agreement to be wed.

In many ways, the legality of marriage has become both a blessing and a hindrance. Any time the courts are involved, power is taken away from the individuals and placed into the hands of someone who may not know the whole story of both parties involved. With the document of legal marriage comes heavy obligations, expectations and ownership; rather than individuals making a daily commitment to each other. A piece of paper says they have to abide by those vows or they are in breach of the contract.

Divorce rates are sky-rocketing, which causes one to reflect upon the ancestors' way of doing things being simpler, not to mention less costly. Money rather than land has become the weapon of power. Not only do marriages cost more in today's world but to end one costs an outrageous amount. Skadi and Njord made a mutual decision to accept the marriage (as defined at that time period) and they chose to make the mutual decision to dissolve that union. The difference really comes down to respect, which is why I think their union is so important to witness and why their end of union is all the more powerful.

Can two people walk away from each other and still remain friends and be respectful of the choices both made mutually? One would hope so. As a married person myself, the institution of marriage and all that comes with that, from the expectations to gender roles and obligations, are things that I have resisted so much that ten years ago we went through an energetic divorce and ditched the titles that imply ownership, such as husband and wife.

Marriage is no picnic and certainly it is not what is portrayed in fairytales or Disney movies. Marriage is hard, frustrating but can be glorious. There is a certain kind of magic that happens when two complete strangers begin to formulate an affection and a desire for each other that leads to a union. Two individuals coming together to share space, time, energy and each other is beautiful. Sometimes those individuals thrive and their differences really complement each other and their union is strengthened, other times it's just *"too much"*. Just like the brisk cold and howling of wolves was too much for Njord, the rocking waves and bitter screech of seagulls was too much for Skadi. This was accepted by them both and others.

Viking unions were a very big event and usually took great time and length in planning. After all, these unions symbolized two different families coming together to form not only a marriage but an alliance. These ceremonies were very business-like, a contract between the two families. Months were spent preparing for the event, with both families very involved in the prepping and investing equally.

Big feasts were had; along with celebrations, dancing, bonfires and plenty of merriment. Everything done in preparation was symbolic and marked a transition from single to married. Ceremonies typically took place in the fall months as this was the harvest season and a time of great abundance. A good harvest ensured a large feast!

The brides were adorned with flower crowns while the grooms were gifted family heirloom weapons. Arm rings as well as wedding rings were exchanged. Toasts of ale and mead were made to the Gods Odin & Freya for blessings of fertility, loyalty and peace. Gifts of honey and mead (which is made from honey) were gifted to the couple as a way of blessing their marriage. This honey gift tradition gave rise the common term we know as "honeymoon."

Within the realm of marriage, running the household was a partnership where both worked equally to ensure the abundance of the homestead. While the men often went away to explore and battle, it was not uncommon for the wife to also make the journey. If children were in the home then the wife often stayed and managed the entire homestead on her own – not an easy task. Men died in battle or were lost at sea.

Divorce was common and women could initiate a divorce for many reasons, such as unhappiness, abuse or poverty. While a woman was bound to be faithful to her husband, the husband was well within his rights to engage with other women; having concubines and even other wives. Men could father numerous children with numerous women but if a woman stepped out of her marriage bounds then she could be killed alongside her lover.

While men certainly had their elevated rights, women too had their own distinct elevations. Women could own property, fight as shield maidens and practice the art of Seidr (*say-der*) – a type of Norse magic and form of shamanism. It is known that few men practiced this art, due to it being primarily a women's practice. Odin himself was rumored to have learned and practiced Seidr, having been taught by Freya. We are seeing a modern-day resurgence in women rising up and leading Asatru/heathen rites in Seidr style. One such renowned woman (and an acquaintance) who has really paved the way for others to follow suit is Diana Paxson.

It is unfair to compare the gender roles we have today with the gender roles of the Viking Age. Women had rights, yes. Women were also property, used to solidify bonds between two families through the contract of marriage. We live in different times and any comparison would be impractical. There are pros and cons, things that worked and things that didn't. Ultimately, all we can do is look at the past and hopefully learn a thing or two.

With marriage being deemed an institution rather than a mutual longing and commitment, it's hard to imagine the concept of happy-ever-after as being practical, let alone realistic. Mervyn Cadwallader, a professor of sociology, posed this vital question: "Why not permit a flexible contract, perhaps for one or two years, with period options to renew? If a couple grew disenchanted with their life together, then they would not feel trapped for life. They would not have to anticipate and then go through the destructive agonies of divorce. They would not have to carry about the stigma of marital failure, like the mark of Cain on their foreheads. Instead of a declaration of war, they could simply let their contract lapse and, while still friendly, be free to continue their romantic quest."

This is why Njord and Skadi's marriage is so vital to look at. Where did we go wrong as a society in institutionalizing marriage and making it a burden to dissolve; a failure to acknowledge that one or both individual's needs, ideals and wants were not being fulfilled? Why in society are we crucified for ending a marital union?

Njord and Skadi's marriage has been given the title "sacred union" by many. This, in my opinion, is pretty accurate. It is sacred in the fact that they both retained their autonomy (defined as the "right or condition of self-government.") In a relationship, autonomy refers to owning, expressing one's deeply personal awareness of needs, interests and values.

Our autonomy in a relationship separates us from the title of who we are in the relationship. What would you consider your core aspects to be, outside of your titles of spouse, parent, friend, sibling? Can you achieve balance between intimacy and autonomy?

This balancing act is not easy! There is a fine tipping of scales in one direction or the other that ultimately causes imbalance. For example, if you have two people who are so invested in the marriage that they sacrifice and give up their autonomy for the sake of the union, then resentment, bitterness and lackluster tip the scale towards an unhappy union. On the other hand, if you have two people who are so deeply invested in preserving their autonomy that neither can meet in the middle and formulate some kind of commonality, then the scale tips again.

In the case of Skadi and Njord, both were already strong in their autonomy and both knew what was going to work and not work. Needs were honestly expressed and the union ended on a good note rather than a battle, like we see most divorces resulting in today. There was no forcing of expectations and compromising one's self for the greater good of the marriage. This kind of real honesty is what elevates their union as sacred, at least in my opinion.

FINDING AUTONOMY WITHIN YOUR RELATIONSHIPS:

List-making and journaling are wonderfully simple tools that allow individuals time to really digest and process emotional things that are occurring. When we take the time to write down things and read them, we are shifting our focus towards inner work rather than projection. In making the following lists, give yourself power to step away from your title within the relationship you are processing:

- **Make a list of your individual talents.**
- **Make a list of your unique accomplishments.**

- Write down ten of your individual interests.
- Who are the people in your life that encourage and support you?
- What are your wants for independence?
- What are your needs for closeness?
- Can you allow your partner to express their wants & needs?

Understanding who you are as an individual and allowing yourself to honor that individuality sets the stage for you allowing the same in your relationships. This is the first step in really building a friendship within your relationship. As a society, we seem to be more accepting of our friends little quirks rather than those of our intimate relationships.

Something dangerous happens in relationships when autonomy is threatened. This concept of "50/50, we are a team, we are one unit" is not really healthy. We are forced to compromise who we are for the comfort of our partner, which can and typically does create resentment. When we can show up as individuals and respect the differences in our partner then we can create a very powerful union. However, this mindset has to be embraced by both involved! It can't be one-sided. In a relationship, neither individual should have to give up their independence, ideals, beliefs or hobbies. You don't always have to be on the same page in a book in order to enjoy the book. The same goes for relationships. You don't always have to do everything together, have the same interests or beliefs in order to enjoy the relationship.

In a wolf pack, there is primarily a lead male and lead female. With the term "alpha" being misused and outdated, these two are commonly referred to as the mated pair or parent wolves. This pair makes up the pack, in other words: they birth the pack. They may have siblings which are the aunts and uncles of the pack but this pair is at the top.

Mated pairs typically mate for life. Attaching terminology that applies to humans, such as monogamous, is pretty unrealistic and unfair as that term means something different for humans and we can't project our ideals onto the animal kingdom. While a mated pair appears to only mate with each other, in order for the survival of the pack to continue it is not unheard of for the parent wolves to mate with other wolves within the pack.

Wolves are social animals, they are highly intelligent and in order for a wolf pack to not only survive but thrive they have to have pups that they collectively raise. Wolf pups raised within the pack structure live a longer, healthier and more abundant life than those whose pack is interrupted by hunters who kill key members of the pack. It is often common for the lead male to have two lead females that he mates with.

In the wolf pack, it is the lead female that runs things. She is, after all, the one that births the pack. Even the lead male, while larger than the female, will ensure her safety and survival. If one of the parent wolves dies, there is a period of grieving. There are stories of the Yellowstone wolf packs where a lead female was trapped and killed. The lead male searched and searched for her, he spent hours trying to free her from the trap and when she was killed, he mourned. Eventually, he would choose to die on the same spot where she died.

Wolves are deeply expressive and highly emotional. They are bonded by loyalty, love and devotion. In the book *Wolfsong* by Catherine Feher-Elson, she states that: "Wolf is one of the most efficient and elegant creations. To understand wolf, one must enter a world of primeval beauty, a world where life and death are inextricably linked. Wolf's world is a land of shadow and light, of love and terror, of forest, plain, desert and tundra – a world of beauty and power where family, pack and clan are the primary focus of life; an ancient world of sacred bonds between predator and prey. Wolf walks in a legend between myth and reality. The call of the wolf on a clear, cold night is an invitation to enter this world."

Scientist who study them have been doing their best to educate the public on the importance of wolves as not just sacred allies to the environment, as they keep things in balance, but as mirrors to humans on how best work together and ensure our survival. Unfortunately, humans are full of ego and most have completely lost their connection to Nature in this concrete world of domination that has been embraced.

When looking to wolves as mirrors for relationships, one can see the amount of love they have for each other with their constant cuddles, play and affection. Parent wolves are unique individuals; they do not force each other to compromise themselves for the other; they mutually care for one another. They provide for each other and the pack. They hunt together, sleep together and communicate clearly. As humans, we are capable of all those things, but ego, pride and a bit of narcissism gets in the way of even the healthiest relationships.

Wolves, like all animals, naturally possess autonomy. They know who they are. They know what they need in order to survive. They are not influenced like humans are. As humans, we struggle trying to fit in. In the Animal Kingdom, each species has its place, attributes and individualities.

I often think of Skadi as the Northern Rocky Mountain timber wolf, preferring her home in the forest; and Njord the Wolf of the Sea, found in the Great Bear Rainforest on the Pacific Coast of Canada, who prefers the waters. Both are unique individuals who have their own needs and prefer their own landscapes. They respect each other but do not demand that the other compromise themselves for the union. They chose to honor each other's autonomy and still remain friends.

CHAPTER TEN

Eyes of the Wolf

"Watch, witness, observe your thoughts – without any judgment, without any condemnation or evaluation ..."
– Rajneesh

There is a saying amongst the native tribes of the world: "If you want to know where the wolves are, simply look to the skies and follow the ravens." As a constant student and one who has devoted the past decade to researching and understanding wolf as messenger, mirror and god, one thing has always stood out in surprise for me and that is that every single book, article, movie or documentary about them all feature pages, chapters, paragraphs, time and energy to a particular corvid: the raven.

Ravens and wolves have the most intensely beautiful relationship. A connection that no one knows when it first began, it just always has been. This ancient kinship, though surprising (due to both being drastically different species), has gifted us mere humans with insight, lessons and magick.

In the book, *Praise for Wolves*, R.D. Lawrence calls this: "Interspecies communion – a mere haunting, spiritual and primitive wild primordial relationship." Wolves rely upon ravens, and ravens rely upon wolves. They seem to always be with each other. Some of the oldest clans and tribes saw this interaction and created the Wolf Clan and Raven Clan, with one or even both of the animals as their totem(s).

In my first book, *Animals as Gods,* I devoted an entire chapter to raven. Theses majestic and often misunderstood or rather unappreciated corvids have been active participants in my life since we moved into our home over twenty years ago. It's hard to dismiss something so beautiful when it literally flies over my head every day!

Ravens are seers. They are known as messengers between the living realm and the spirit realm. They share similar attributes found within the myths of the coyote, as both are known to be mischievous, mysterious, and unpredictable and they are often called the tricksters. They know the past, the present and the future. In many of the creation myths it is said that raven is responsible for creating the land, plants, humans and animals. Raven created all animals to have duality – a good side and a not-so-good side.

One animal in particular was created for a specific reason. According to the Athabascan people of the Pacific Northwest: "Raven decided to create an animal that could be a teacher for the humans. Raven covered this animal with fur, made it stand on four feet and filled it with intelligence, strength, courage and compassion. Raven provided the animal with a long snout, sharp teeth and a very powerful sense of smell. Raven created wolves. Raven taught the wolves how to hunt, to howl and to follow the other ravens which would show them where the game was so they could feast together. This first wolf family was very happy, their children and grandchildren roamed the lands. The descendants of these first wolves survive today and they continue to share the world with humans. It is as it always was: wolves are willing to share life with humans and other beings as well." – Catherine Feher-Elson.

Not only do ravens and wolves actually feast together but they continue to work together in finding food. Ravens will let wolves know where good meat is; wolves will tear open the thick flesh and allow ravens to share the meal. Ravens have been spotted nesting above wolves' dens and even filling the role of nanny to the wolf pups. Ravens are one of the first playmates for the pups. These acts are voluntary and have earned the ravens the title of "Wolf Birds".

Ravens, like wolves, are masters of communication. They have learned to recognize the many different howls of the wolves and the wolves in return have learned to recognize and discern what each raven call means. Together they have found a way to not only survive amongst each other but thrive.

Raven is bringer of magic, an omen and, as creator, one who transforms. As messenger, raven delivers word from the beyond or the cosmos. Odin, the "Allfather" of the Norse gods, is said to have two ravens – Hugin & Mugin, whose names mean "thought" and "memory". These birds are his messengers that are sent out each morning, fly all over the world and deliver back to him their findings.

In Old Norse there were women who were known as "Volva" (which translates into seeress, shaman or witch) who practiced the art of Seidr (say-ther) – a form of divination magic. Some believe that this practice stems from the early aboriginal people – the Sami's – who neighbored the Norse. Seidr worked through trance and ecstatic movement by the main Volva who enters an elevated state of mind while sitting or laying on a raised platform. She would enter a trance which would allow her to see as a clairvoyant to divine the future, heal the sick, control the weather, sway a battle, solve disputes or bring luck and blessings to the crops. A tool that was often utilized in these workings was a staff which, in the twelfth century throughout Europe and the UK, was something that became outlawed to even own.

Skadi is mentioned briefly as being a seeress who, side-by-side with Freya, could enter a trance-like state and see into the past, present and future. It is Freya who is believed to have taught not only Skadi this mostly feminine art but also Odin himself. Who really knows for certain? Skadi does come from a very powerful bloodline, with her father being a well-known shapeshifter and worker of great magic himself – some things could have been handed down.

What we do know is that Skadi lived atop a great mountain giving her a bird's-eye-view of all below. In the book *Baldr's Magic*, the author, Nicholas E. Brink, mentions that Skadi, along with Freya, "could see and hear into the future." It is believed that through trance Skadi could see the outcome of battles and warn of potential death or defeat. Raven sightings have often been interpreted as omens of death or defeat in battles. This is partly due to the fact that ravens scavenge the battlefields and would gather in a mass or "murder" to consume the dead.

Going back to the creation myth where raven created humans and animals, giving them polarity, we could be so bold as to say that Skadi mirrors the polarity of raven and wolf attributes. As seeress, she protects and offers guidance to her people by sharing perspective and insight. As wolf, she offers us loyalty, strength and warrior attributes. When we look to Skadi as mirroring these diverse animal attributes, it becomes easier to relate to her on a personal level and allow those attributes to surface in ourselves. We can give light to our own inner polarities.

The Hopi people believe that: "All of life is one life, the same." They believe that all things, rocks, trees, plants, birds, bugs, animals and humans all contain a spark, an essence, a divine spirit. This spark is called "kachi" which means "spirit". This belief of the divine, a spirit, is directly connected to animism, which is the belief that objects, places and all creatures possess a spiritual essence. When we begin to adopt this belief or enhance our already existent practice, it is very easy to see that we share similar attributes with animals such as ravens and wolves. Sometimes it takes a Giant such as Skadi to be the one to mirror them to us.

Skadi displays *wolf* loyalty to her father when she bursts into Odin's great hall and demands justice for his untimely death. She also displays *raven* discernment when she takes time to ponder Odin's proposition of a different solution. With wolf and raven being such incredible companions, not only in the wild, we can see how they can be fluid in one as an individual – polarity in action.

Life is not so black and white, cut-and-dried. It is unhealthy to be imbalanced into only one way of being. In fact, it is quite impossible. We humans are filled with polarities. We may not like them and those around us may find them to be a bit hypocritical in their method of being displayed, but we cannot deny that they are there.

Wolves are known for their ability to be quick and sharp to act. They can take down prey at an unnerving speed. As apex predators, they are at the top of the food chain, with no natural predators (with the exception of humans). We are the main predator and unfortunately we have forgotten that the animals have been our teachers since the beginning of time. Hopefully, we can remedy this harmful arrogance.

Wolves are loyal and deeply devoted to the survival of their family pack. Everything a wolf does is anchored into its family's needs, despite the portrayal that the media and films show us.

Ravens have been known as messengers that obtain their findings through observation and listening skills. Corvids in general spend quite a bit of their life in active flight. From above, they observe in fine detail everything below. Their eyesight is incredibly sharp and they remember things. For example, when I wear my hair down while outside, the ravens perched nearby know that I am the one that will leave them food. When my hair is tied up, they fly in closer so that they can see my face. One way we can begin to embrace raven attributes within ourselves is to really lean into our skills of observation.

What if, instead of immediately attacking someone in self-defense, we stop and observe with a new perspective and ask ourselves: is this really worth time and energy? Learning to observe without judgment is a difficult task in this world where we are encouraged, taught and expected to see others as our competition – to take them down and dominate! While some would assume that this "conquer, destroy and battle" way of thinking is a wolf trait, they would be wrong. Yes, wolves may be apex predators; however, they do not kill simply for the sake of it, nor do they always fight with aggression. I cannot say the same for humans.

We can all honor our inner wolf and raven. While our ego brain may want to rationalize this connection, our intuitive brain will allow us to feel it better through a meditation that is meant to assist you in connecting with both raven and wolf attributes.

WOLF TO RAVEN SHAPESHIFTING MEDITATION

Allow your eyes to gently close as you bring your awareness to your breath.

Take a nice deep inhale and exhale fully. Breathe in and breathe out.

Observe how your physical body relaxes each time you exhale, for it is impossible to be tense when you are exhaling. Give yourself permission to relax your forehead, your mouth and your jaw as you simply continue to breathe in and breathe out. Feel that relaxation move down your neck, your shoulders, your arms, all the way down to your fingertips. Feel as that heavy relaxation moves down to your chest, your stomach and your hips, moving down to your thighs, your calves and your feet.

Here you sit completely physically relaxed.

Bring your focus deeper into your breath.

Take a nice deep inhale … 2 … 3 … 4 … and out … 2 … 3 … 4 …

(Repeat three times)

Now breathing at your own pace, breathing fully and easily, your body creates a natural rhythm as you simply breathe in and breathe out.

In your mind's eye, feel yourself tucked in comfortably inside a very warm den.

The den is covered with fur and it is incredibly warm.

You begin to feel as though you are curled up in an almost fetal position. You feel very warm.

Breathing into this den, where it is very dark, you begin to activate your sense of smell.

Breathing in deeply you smell dirt – musky and moist. You smell fur. You are smelling yourself ...

Here in the dark in the den, with your sense of smell activated, you begin to move and stretch, only your legs are not human legs, neither are your arms. As you stretch, your eyes have adjusted to the darkness and you see fur, everywhere, all over you. Your feet and hands are now paws, with thick padding. You have claws where you once had nails. Give yourself permission to activate and connect with this new form here in the dark. This musky, fur covered animal you know to be wolf.

(Pause)

Let yourself stretch more and more, move around until you are outside of the den. Feel the Sun as you stand on all four limbs, connect with the grass beneath your paws and breathe in deeply and breathe out, letting some of your breath escape through your teeth, feeling your lips vibrate. With each breath your senses are heightened and you can smell so intensely that you feel a pull to go towards whatever scent has caught your attention. Feel and see as you dig your claws into the grass, finding the dirt beneath. When you are ready run, run, run! You can go so fast! With all four fur covered legs, you are running faster than you have ever run before.

You feel completely free, wild and untamed, running towards a scent drifting on the wind.

It doesn't even matter what you are smelling, you are enjoying the run so much!

The freedom.

The wild. This you!

Bring your run to a stop and feel once more the earth beneath your paws.

Bring your nose down to the grass and breathe in the dirt and crisp grass. With your snout to the ground you slowly begin to shed wolf energy. You begin to cock your head in a slow and strategic manner. Your canine snout becomes thicker, harder, longer and pointed. You begin to grow a beak.

Feel as your breath changes and the way you breathe changes as you move your beak closer to the ground, almost pressing into the ground. Looking down at your paws, you see that they have become talons; sharp piercing claws on rough, scaled legs.

Your body and weight begin to shift as you become much smaller, feeling the weight shift from your front to your back talons. Your once front legs and paws are now almost weightless, they begin to stretch out to the side where they are covered with feathers - dark, black shining feathers.

Your entire body is now that of raven. Breathe that in. Breathe in the mystery and intellect of this wise bird. Feel yourself move on the ground, almost in a hopping manner as you move your taloned feet that grasp the grass, holding the dirt. When you are ready, hop up a little higher, as if your talons are kicking off the ground. Keep hopping until your wings join you and you take flight. Feel as your wings catch the breeze and lift you higher and higher. Feel as you glide in the air, gazing below at the landscape. You are weightless. You cock your head and see with new eyes, a new perspective.

(Pause)

Slowly bring yourself back down to the ground. Bring your focus back to your breath.

Begin to stretch your talons until they become human feet and legs once more – your feet and your legs. Feel your wings stretch until they once again become your arms and hands. Feel your entire body shake the feathers off, revealing your skin beneath, activating your internal organs as you breathe back into your physical human form. Do the same with your face, feeling your beak become small, flesh-covered, along with your lips, eyelids and cheeks.

Breathe in your whole, complete and invigorated form back to human.

Here you sit, fully recharged with the energy of wolf, intuition activated with the energy of raven.

Give thanks to wolf for stamina, strength and the ability to flee when necessary or to charge when warranted. Give thanks to raven for being weightless, rising above and seeing with a new perspective, for knowing when to sink your talons deep and when to soar onward.

Slowly begin to wiggle your fingers and toes, begin to become aware of your surroundings.

Breathing into every cell, bone and muscle an awakening. Feeling your arms and legs begin to stretch.

Taking another deep breath in and exhaling fully.

When you are ready, open your eyes and come back to this space.

Allow yourself some time to process the meditation. You may find it helpful to write down in a journal your responses to the following questions:

- Did you find it easier to connect with one animal more than the other? Why do you think this is?
- Were you more comfortable running on land?
- Were you more at home flying in the sky?
- When raven came through, which attributes did you feel a connection with?

- When wolf came through, which attributes did you feel a connection with?
- Can you see the polarity within you?

Whether you connected more with raven or more with wolf, what I want you to gain from this meditation experience is that within you is both, and within others is both! Respect and honor those divine, sentient and wholesomely unique attributes in each other. Ravens and wolves are drastically different species! Each human being is drastically different from every other. If ravens and wolves have managed to live amongst each other harmoniously then we as humans should be able to do the same!

If Skadi was able to soften her intense desire for revenge and live amongst those whom she deemed responsible for killing her kin, why can't we *mere humans* learn to get along? What is it going to take for us to be okay with agreeing to disagree and still be civil? When are we going to allow others to be themselves and stop demanding that they conform to what we expect or wish them to be so that we can feel comfortable? Society is broken and a big reason why is that we have disconnected from our natural world. We have modern conveniences that have made it easy for us to forget what our ancestors did and who they learned from.

Ravens are the eyes of the wolf. They are the messengers. They have always been the teachers. In our lives, we are not solo students. We are constantly learning from someone or something else, whether that be an actual teacher, online, or an animal. There are lessons being given that we simply need to open our eyes to see. Maybe we just need to look up?!

In April of 2022, I led a three day, three night weekend for women, devoted to ravens as being the eyes of the wolf. Anchoring deep into animism and animals as teachers has created profound change in not only my life but those who circle with me. What I witnessed was transformation as each woman realized that she can activate both attributes of wolf and raven.

As a pack of wild women, we were able to sit and be taught, not just by the priestesses who were offering workshops, but we were also taught by each other, by the land and by the animals that visited us each day, ravens being one of those visitors.

There are times in life where we all need to be more like a wolf; tend to our pack, watch, observe, run into action or simply enjoy each other's company. There are times where we all need to be more like raven; watch instead of react, shift perspective, soar above the drama and keep our loved-ones safe. Together, wolves and ravens mirror our own inner polarities and make them something to honor rather than hide away from.

Animism, for me, is the ability to see, honor and respect all things as living, breathing, divine and sentient beings. In a world that feeds us division, labels, judgments, criticism and competition, this mindset can be difficult at first. Recently I attended a lunch where my friend invited her two circles to sit at one table. At first, what I observed and heard were old competitive patterns, one-upping and some open criticism mixed with shameful judgments. It felt very *high school*.

In my efforts to not participate, I closed my eyes, took a deep breath and asked *"source"* to help me open up to a greater sight; to be able to see each person as a reflection of their spirit animal. When I opened my eyes, I saw a zoo sitting at the table. This was my "aha" moment. We are all so unique and it is natural to want to express our unique selves in the presence of other unique selves.

When we view each other as animals, we can rid ourselves of that human ego mindset. We can start to create a shift and really start to love, honor and allow each individual to simply sit at our table. Wolves and ravens have been a symbiotic pair since the beginning of time. They have found a way to survive and thrive together. Skadi found a way to survive and thrive within Odin's hall and eventually make a home amongst the other gods and still honor her individuality. Skadi is both Mother of Wolves and

Raven Messenger. She mirrors to us the polarity of an individual who is a strong, capable and fierce warrior – all wolf attributes and yet she maintains her mystery, keen observation and incredible intellect as raven.

"I am a raven who flies with the wolves; you are a raven who flies with the wolves.

We are all ravens flying with wolves, flying, flying ravens with wolves."

CHAPTER ELEVEN

Wolves in Norse Mythology

The Norse sagas are filled with wolves. These creatures are key figures and players in the myths and legends that we have come to love and embrace so much. With Skadi as *Mother of Wolves* and *Great Defender*, it would be natural for her to see both the good and bad in all, especially in wolves. But she is not the only parent of wolves. Odin is known as Father of Wolves. Loki is also known as Father of Wolves. It would be unfair to mention the children without mentioning the fathers. One thing I have learned in my years of practice is to give credit where credit is due, especially when it is the Allfather himself who created the wolves in the beginning. It was always the Allfather.

It is said that after Odin Allfather and his brother's, Ve and Vili, made the world, Odin traveled. After some time, Odin was lonely, so he created two wolves and named them Geri and Freki.

Odin wanted companionship and help with his hunting. His wolves were constantly by his side.

Odin loved the beauty and affection of his wolves. With his two wolves he was no longer lonely.

All of the world's wolves are the children of Odin's wolves.

Odin One-eyed also created the first two ravens and named them Hugin and Munin (thought and memory). Each dawn he would send out his ravens, one to the east and one to the west, to gather insight and news of the world.

Each evening the ravens would return and relay the knowledge they saw and heard back to Odin.

The wolves and ravens were children of Odin, which made them siblings. They were kith, kin, clan, tribe and family. The wolves would make the kill and share their feast with the ravens.

Today, wolves and ravens are still seen together.

When Odin made the first man and first woman, he told them to look to the skies and follow the ravens to the teachers of the land; the wolves. Wolves, Odin said, will teach you how to hunt, to communicate and to live together peacefully.

Could the wolf association be what softened the tension between Skadi and Odin when she erupted into his great hall demanding justice? Was it her battle cry for vengeance? Her loyalty to kith and kin? Something about her struck Odin and in her prowess he welcomed her into his pack. Skadi lived amongst the gods as a goddess. It is rumored that she and Odin were lovers and had children of their own. This union would only solidify her more as *Mother of Wolves*.

As a mother myself, fighting to the death for my children is not even a question. If it is needed than as a mother I will rise. Children, like wolves, are individuals; they contain polarities, inner dualities and conflict. No one here is perfect animal or human! My children's flaws or shortcomings are theirs to honor, embrace and reshape; not mine!

Growing up in a very staunch religious State, we were taught the opposite: that the children's actions are a direct reflection of the parents. As a rebellious teenager, I was often asked: "What will people think of me as your parent?" Thank the goddess this mindset has changed within my mother with age and wisdom.

Children are individuals who must stumble and fall, rise and run because of their own choosing. My mother has allowed all her six children to do just that, she no longer anchors into guilt or shame that society has thrust upon her – she allows, she loves. Both my parents are excellent human beings that have raised my siblings and I to be imperfectly authentic souls who live our lives to the fullest.

The wolves in Norse sagas are also individuals who must make choices, suffer consequences and ultimately mirror to those who see into the depths of the stories and myths the lessons therein. One of my favorite quotes is from the Disney movie *Brave*: "Legends are lessons – they ring with truth." To read a myth is to not just graze over the words but to become consumed by the hidden insights, to dig deeper and uncover those sparks that ignite passionate triggers.

It is said that in the beginning Odin gifted Sol, the Sun God, and Mani, the God of the Moon, two chariots possessing great speed. These chariots would allow Sol and Mani to travel across the sky once each day, bringing light during the day and light during the night.

However, these two gods were distracted easily and tended to wander off course, causing a great imbalance amongst the humans, who did not know when to sleep and when to wake.

Odin became outraged with their distractions and wanted to thrust his mighty spear at them.

Seeing his frustration, Loki offered a solution.

Loki convinced the wolves Skoll and Hati to chase the Sun and Moon Gods throughout the skies with the promise that if they were ever able to catch them then they could eat them in one bite.

Out of fear of these two great wolves eating them, Sol and Mani remained on course, returning day and night to a normal rhythm.

Skoll – "One who mocks" (also known as "deception"). This is the wolf that chases the Sun, according to Icelandic historian, Snorri

Sturluson. In the Grimnismal "Eddic poem", *Skoll is the name of the wolf that follows the shining priest into the desolate forest, and the other is Hati Hrodvitnir's son, who chases the bright bride of the sky.* This stanza suggests the opposite, that Skoll hunts the Moon and Hati the Sun. With the prey of Skoll being masculine and the prey for Hati being female, we can safely conclude that in Norse mythology as the Moon is masculine, Skoll would chase the Moon. The Sun is feminine, so Hati would chase the Sun.

Hati– "One who hates" (also known as "hate"). This is the wolf that chases the Moon, according to Icelandic historian, Snorri Sturluson. However, again there are some contradictions and confusions and no one really knows for certain. There is some speculation that these two wolves are sons of Fenrir the Wolf (who brings about the dreaded end of the gods reign: "Ragnarok"), which would be why Loki was able to command them, as he is the father of Fenrir, so he would be acting as grandfather in demanding that Skoll and Hati keep Sol and Mani on track by chasing them. Both Skoll and Hati are pivotal in the bringing about of Ragnarok. Myth explains that they must swallow the Moon and Sun, bringing about worldwide darkness, which instigates Ragnarok.

Contradictions and misinterpretations are rampant when it comes to decoding what the Norse really practiced; this is due in part to oral traditions rather than written. No one really knows for certain who did what exactly. All we have are historians who do their best to translate to their upmost capabilities. When it comes to working with any of the Old Ones, it is best to formulate a guttural connection, to ask yourself: what feels right for you? While there may be some that argue this with me, my personal connection with the Old Ones is just that: personal. So if it works for me – it works! As I am no scholar and do not remember in detail my past lives and personal connections with these Old

Ones, I can simply do my best to connect with them in this life with what limited information there is available.

If Loki is grandfather and Fenrir father, then who is mother of these two wolves? It is believed by Snorri Sturluson that in the *Volupsa* (one of the Poetic Eddas, dating back to the tenth century) it is mentioned that these two wolves were birthed by a Giantess or witch – a seeress who bore many, all in wolf-form. While her actual name is not known, there are always assumptions that can be made. Could the mother be one of Skadi's ancestors from the Land of Giants?

What we do know is that Skoll and Hati possessed long, sharp and deadly fangs that could rip apart anything. They had claws so sharp they could cut through the thickest metal with a simple touch. Their speed was indescribable and their stamina unbeatable. These are two wolves that endure much in their task to chase Sol and Mani day and night. In their pursuit, they chase without food or rest – simply for the chase! Without them, we would not have balance – our days would be endless nights and our nights endless days.

Let's go back to the creation myth where Odin, seeking companionship, created the first two wolves – a male and a female, Geri and Freki. These two wolves were the first teachers for the humans. Similar to the Native Tribes' creation myth where Spirit Raven, seeking assistance to help bless the land and teach the humans, created wolves to be those teachers. It is interesting that raven is the great creator. Ravens are sacred birds to Odin and, as Great Shapeshifter, Odin himself could shift into raven form. Was it Odin all along, was he Spirit Raven?

These wolves were highly esteemed and honored. They were known to assist the Valkyries in leading the fallen and chosen warriors to Odin's great hall. They were his companions, who feasted amongst the gods. The connection between Odin and his wolves inspired many. As leader and Father of Wolves, he was and is part wolf. Odin has warriors called Ulfhednar who in a frenzy could shift into wolves much like the Berserkers who could shift into bears; another one of Odin's animals which he could shift into. In wolf form, Odin could wander with great speed and in his travels we know that Odin enjoyed the company of women, so he created children in wolf form called Volsungs who inherited the ability to shapeshift into wolves. Thus we have those warriors who still to this day proclaim to be one of Odin's wolves.

Geri – (Which translated means "greedy" or "greed") and *Freki* – (translated as "ravenous" or "hungry") sit on each side of Odin. One is black and one is white. One is female and one is male. They are the yin and the yang that bring about balance.

Together, these two wolves symbolize wisdom; they offer protection and inspire bravery. When one sleeps, the other remains awake so that a watchful pair of eyes is always alert. They are creatures of duality in the flesh, mirroring to all good, bad, kind, cruel, destruction and solace.

It is mentioned in the Eddas that Odin does not eat, what food he has at his feasts he gives to his two wolves. Odin created Hugin and Munin, his ravens, to help him hunt and thus feed his wolves. Odin is known to survive on wine alone as wine is "both meat and drink."

Wolf medicine and magic is anchored into earth, this physical and tangible realm, while ravens are air, intellect and insight. It is fascinating that the Allfather is both earth anchored and air inspired with his sacred animals.

Fenrir – Mighty bringer of the twilight of the gods, marsh dweller, he who is son of the trickster. Poor Fenrir! In my heart I carry a soft spot for this mighty wolf who is the son of Loki and Angrboda, the seeress who showed Odin many things, including Ragnarok. Fenrir is given a heavy weight to carry with one of his many names and titles being "Vanargand" which translates as "creature of expectation." Fenrir is doom-bringer and his weight is his fate.

Fenrir is one of Loki's monsters, his children, who were abused and mistreated by the gods out of fear of a prophecy. Fenrir was not a monster from the beginning. He lived peacefully as a beloved pet until betrayal triggered him to defend not only himself but his siblings. Fenrir is brother to Hel and the great serpent Jormungandr, all whom were birthed by Angrboda (who is quite frankly not given the credit she deserves), commonly known as simply the Mother of Monsters (on a side note, please read *The Witches Heart* by Genevieve Gornichec, as she gives Angrboda her due credit).

Out of fear that the prophecy of Ragnarok would come about, there were some precautions taken, rather harshly and rashly. First, Odin thrust the great serpent Jormungandr into the sea. Hel was sent to Niflhel, the realm of ice, where she was given the responsibility of welcoming the sick and dying souls. Fenrir was taken as a pet! That is, until he began to grow at an alarming rate, which triggered fear and served as a reminder of what Fenrir was capable of doing, if prophecy was to be fulfilled.

Fenrir is bound with a chain called Dromi, which is supposed to be unbreakable! To test this theory, the gods taunt and test Fenrir, teasing him that he cannot, despite his size and strength, break this chain. Fenrir breaks this chain easily, which only furthers the fear.

So Odin, not wanting to die as revealed in prophecy, demands that Fenrir be bound with something that is actually unbreakable. He reaches out the Dwarves through a messenger. They go to their forge and create a chain called *Gleipnir*, which translates as *Entangler*. This chain is said to have been made from six ingredients: "cat's footsteps, woman's beard, mountain roots, bear sinew, fish breath and spittle of birds."

Fenrir is tricked! He is invited to join the gods on the island of Lyngvi to test his strength on a new chain. The gods once again tease and taunt him. He is shown a thin band of a chain and told that he cannot break it. Fenrir doesn't see honor in breaking something so small and delicate, so he will only agree if one of the gods will put their hand in his mouth during the test of strength. Tyr the Warrior God accepts this challenge and places his hand within Fenrir's mouth.

Fenrir is bound. He cannot break from the delicate looking chain. He struggles. The more he struggles, the tighter the chain becomes. Fenrir is trapped. A betrayal. In his anger and pain, he closes his jaws upon Tyr and removes Tyr's hand. The gods all laugh at their trickery, except Tyr who now has no hand! They thrust a sword into Fenrir's mouth, forcing it to remain open. Then they bind the unbreakable chain to a large stone, which is bound to an even larger stone. Fenrir is left on the island.

Skoll and Hati, Fenrir's sons, leave their charge in the sky after finally catching their prey. The twilight of the gods, the endless night and winter begin. Skoll and Hati attempt to save their father, but even their sharp claws and fangs cannot break the unbreakable chain. They are captured and thrust into a cell for safe keeping. Fenrir eventually breaks free and swallows everything in his path, including Odin. Ragnarok happens regardless of the preventative and cruel measures taken to avoid it.

Despite the prophecy expressed by the seeress or Volva, there were always choices. Despite fate being predetermined, it is up to the individual to ensure that fate through their actions or create their own fate. Did Odin bring about Ragnarok in his attempt to avoid it? What if he hadn't chosen to punish Loki's children for a rumored part that they were foretold they would play? Could Ragnarok have been avoided if Odin and the god's decided to treat Fenrir with kindness? Who wouldn't fight back and defend themselves if they were tethered and bound against their will?

Fenrir is, for me, one of the most powerful wolves in Norse mythology. He represents choices which lead to consequences. There is a reason why Fenrir is tattooed on my leg. To move forward in life despite fear is living as a warrior. Fenrir was tricked, bound and abused by those he grew up to trust. This is not unheard of! He naturally reacted from a place of anger and defense, who wouldn't?

Fenrir mirrors to me a cautious trust in humans who are ruled by fear. He shows me to trust my gut. After all, what if he hadn't gone to the island? What if he hadn't given in to the taunting? He also mirrors to me inner strength. Fenrir didn't need to test his strength in order to be accepted by the gods, he could have just accepted his strength. How often do we do that as humans? We put ourselves in situations where we choose to prove who we are in the hopes of validation and acceptance all the time! Fenrir grew so large and was prophesied to grow even larger. He was seen as a threat, yet he displayed no physical threat until he was betrayed, tricked and bound.

How many times have you seen strong individuals, whose very lives and essence appear giant, taken down, attacked and ridiculed in order to make those attacking feel larger? This happens so much that it has become normal. It's become expected. We often see those around us that are strong in their individuality as threats, as our competition and through patriarchy we are programmed to take them down! To conquer them, to bind them and destroy. Interestingly enough, I see this in women's circles more than I would like – women embracing a patriarchal mindset in the disguise of empowerment.

It all comes from a place of fear. Odin was fearful of his own death. So, out of fear, he did everything in his grasp to avoid it, which still resulted in his death. If our fate of how we are born and how we are to die has already been determined, then the only thing we really have control over is how we live.

Wolves as teachers have been mirroring to us mere humans how to live more consciously and we in our arrogance continue to ignore them. Odin forgot out of fear who he had created to be the teachers. Fenrir could have taught him much had he disconnected from that fear. Thus, the Allfather once again gifts us with insight of his imperfections.

There are some animals that are more profound as teachers, just as there are Old Ones who are more profound as mirrors. It comes down to allowing their attributes to be observed within us as individuals. There are times in my life where I am more Skoll and Hati – running in a chase, racing after what others have told me to run towards; a constant pursuit of the Sun and Moon.

There are times where I am more Geri and Freki, striving for balance within my inner masculine and feminine, seeking to mirror acceptance of my own inner dualities while remaining loyal to my core essence. Then there are times I am more Fenrir, moving forward away from fear, knowing my fate has all but been determined; all but the in-between, which is where I really get to live. Sitting with the choices I made to exert trust, feel betrayal and not react in anger but enter into allowance of the process. Owning my reactions is huge!

Skadi, Odin and Loki as mother and fathers to wolves have given us their children as teachers. Why are we not allowing ourselves to be taught? As a mother, teaching my children the basics for survival in this world is something that I feel every parent must do. However, I have learned that my children teach me more than I have ever taught them. Where was Skadi when Fenrir was tricked and bound? Was she atop her mountain with her wolves, reminding them that they are teachers? Oftentimes, the ones teaching by example are the ones who become bound and blamed by others' projections of victimhood, fear and human insecurities. Her wolves teach us still and yet we are still hunting them.

"Wolves were venerated and worshipped; they were considered divine messengers and even gods! Wolves play an important role in many creation myths; they were and still are the ancestors of many peoples." – Ralph Haussler.

https://ralphhaussler.weebly.com/wolf-deities-and-myths.html

CHAPTER TWELVE

Ceremonies of Devotion

As a ritual priestess, I know that ceremony is the act of connection and offering of devotion. It is the tangible, physical display of devotion and reaching out to the gods, higher power or divine source as is defined by the individual(s) performing the ritual. While there is no right or wrong way to connect, call upon and summon, there are movements, phrases and physical acts that make ceremony personal and empowering. This chapter includes actual rituals and ceremonies that I have moved through individually and offered to my community. They worked for me and hopefully they will serve as an option or idea for you the individual to expand upon and make your own.

Working with the Old Ones, gods, goddesses and animals is a very personal work of devotion and as such should contain language, items and knowledge that you the individual have invested time and energy into. I am no expert, simply a constant student. Some ceremonies were more profound than others, most cannot even be remembered as I was so engaged that they became pure instinct. So please do with this chapter what you will and in the end know that you are the one that is master of your ceremonies.

In the book, *The Children of Ash* and Elm by Neil Price, he discusses the concept of religion practiced during the Viking Age: "The Vikings did not ignore their gods, by any means, and they certainly had rituals of acknowledgement and need, coming to terms with them." In these rituals they often had "spiritual intermediaries" who with training were responsible for directly contacting the gods and relaying their messages back to the people.

We are seeing a resurgence of sacred ceremonies and rites all over the world as more and more people are looking back to the past and embracing Paganism, Wicca and Asatru (a religious sect that attempts to revive ancient Norse religious beliefs and practices of pre-Christian Europe), just to name a few. Our idea and practice of religion cannot fairly be compared to those in the past as, again, we have no written documentation or actual proof that they did consider their practices religious. This word "religion" is something that we have in our modern world created an attachment to.

Religion is: "The belief in and worship of a superhuman controlling power, especially a personal god or gods." How do we really know if those early Scandinavians in the Viking Age actually saw their gods as gods, as we define them to be today? Do we know if they "worshipped" them or are we simply speculating? If we are speculating, what are the sources? Does it even really matter?

We do know that there were buildings that appear to have been used for ceremonial purposes. Excavations have revealed artifacts that clearly were not used in simple domestic dwellings. These buildings have been discovered in Denmark, Norway and Sweden. Neil Price states that these buildings were given the term *horgr*, which translates as a small building or enclosure where rituals were performed to the gods. Another term used is *hov* or *hof*, which means temple-halls.

What kind of rituals were happening and why? Are those who are activating the resurgence of the old ways actually doing similar rites? Again, we live in completely different times. Our battles and needs in no way compare to those of the past. We do not have to fight to maintain land. We do not have to arrange marriages to solidify alliances. Our needs of the gods cannot compare to those of our ancient ancestors. Why then do we see a trend in looking back to the old ways?

It is not my place to speak for others. I can only speak for myself. When I do rituals and ceremonies, they are for my own personal spiritual gain. There is a sense of comfort and peace that helps me to create balance and harmony in my own life. For each ceremony or ritual you perform, there is an intention that comes first. A call to the gods is typically for a specific reason.

Ceremony as defined by the dictionary means:
1. A formal religious or public occasion, typically one celebrating a particular event.
2. The ritual observances and procedures performed at grand and formal occasions.

Ritual is defined as:
1. A religious or solemn ceremony consisting of a series of actions performed according to a prescribed order.
2. Relating to or done as a religious or solemn rite.

Rite is defined as:
1. A religious or other solemn ceremony or act.

Blót is defined as:
1. A ritual sacrifice to the gods, the wights, ancestors.
2. A sacrificial *offering* of blood of animals and sometimes humans.

– "Main Devotional Rite in Norse Paganism"
from *The Way of Fire and Ice* by Ryan Smith.

A common rite that is performed each Yuletide within my communal circles is a Sumbel which, defined by Erich Shall, is: "A formal drinking ritual composed of toasting, hails, oath-taking, the recitation of poetry or song and other forms of verbal expression. The Sumbel is composed of rounds, in which the horn is passed in a circle, each person saying their hail or other appropriate verbal expression, drinking and passing the horn along. The purpose of the Sumbel is great; words spoken at a Sumbel have a great power to them, imbued by the nature of the holy rite. Oath-taking is a common part of Sumbel, as it is considered to be especially meaningful and especially binding to take an oath before the gods and the community during this rite. This rite not only connects us with the gods and goddesses, but with our ancestors, our community and, to a degree, with ourselves. Here we may express ourselves in a holy forum, allowing us to define our place in the community as well as honor the gods and goddesses."

A typical Sumbel can be broken up into four parts:
1. An introduction by whoever is hosting the Sumbel.
2. The first round – dedicated to the gods and goddesses – they are hailed at this time.
3. The second round – dedicated to the ancestors and heroes gone by – they are hailed at this time.
4. The third round – This is the time for all to make oaths, speak poetry, sing a song, etc.

A Sumbel can have many more rounds than three and those rounds are usually "anything goes" as long as what is spoken is in the proper vein and with the spirit of a holy gathering.

A Sumbel usually ends with the pouring out of the horn's remaining drink, much like that which is done at a blót's end. The horn is refilled multiple times during the Sumbel, of course, and is sometimes filled once more for the libation. The rite is then declared at an end. Much of the etiquette held for a blót also applies here.

Ceremony, rituals, blots and Sumbels are physical and spiritual ways to shift consciousness and open yourself up to messages, insight and connection. They are dedicated time and energy that are created with intention and devotion. Ryan Smith says that: "Ritual is a longer spiritual ceremony that includes at least one rite. Rituals are usually longer than individual rites and include other actions, such as offerings, performances, chanting, meditation and whatever else best serves the participants and the ritual's objective."

Ruth Barrett, a Dianic high priestess with over 25 years of experience in teachings and creating rituals, states that: "Ritual provides a form to convey meaning to ourselves through the manipulation of symbolic objects and specific activities or actions. A ritual serves as a bridge to carry purposeful, symbolic meaning to the personal or collective conscious and subconscious mind. Ritual is the language of religion. Ritual can give a sense of connection to our ancestors."

With intention being the first step in crafting a ceremony or ritual that is typically a personal intent or one that is set by the group who is going to perform the rite, there are many ways to conduct and move through ceremony and each way is the right way for the one(s) involved. Energy is vital to keeping a flow that compliments the intention.

In my practice, it has been my deep honor to attend ceremonies that were strictly Wiccan, Dianic, traditional witchcraft, non-denominational and non-Christian. Each ceremony had its own pulse and power. Some were more earth-shaking and spiritual, while others were lacking pizzazz. What I loved about each was that specific time and energy were invested into creating something out of the mundane. There is power when we disconnect from the day-to-day routines and enter a time and space that has been dedicated and set apart for specific intent.

As a ritual priestess, it has been my privilege to lead ceremonies that ranged from baby naming ceremonies, mother's blessings, coming of age, activating justice, healing the sick to blessing the garden, drawing down the Moon, turning the wheel of the seasonal year and much more. Most rituals consisted of an outline and resulted in the outline not being followed, as source or intuition took hold and a new flow was birthed spontaneously. Trusting one's gut and allowing things to unfold and birth in sacred dedicated space creates profound, guttural ceremonies.

While one could simply pick up a book or do a google search to find rituals, the best ones are the ones that flow instinctually. As a student of life and spirituality, I have read, verbatim, rituals from books and the energy did not flow. There was a disconnect. For me, it came down to the fact that I was reading words and reciting phrases that I would not typically use, so things did not flow. While rituals are wonderful ideas when offered in books just like this one, it is wise to formulate your own and simply use if you wish the ones offered as a guide or outline rather than a law to be followed by the letter.

When creating a ceremony or ritual in honor of Skadi, which attributes of her are you wanting to activate? Which runes compliment the intention of the rite and are you calling to Skadi or her aspect of wolves? Maybe you are wanting to awaken the hunter within? Will you call upon her bow, arrows or blade? Sit with your intention and allow ideas to flow.

Many rituals have tools that are used, such as incense, the staff of the Seidr, runes, cauldrons, candles and more. Do you have all the tools that you are wanting to use? Does your ritual even require those? If ritual is the act of connecting with source, as is defined by the practitioner, then really you are the only one that can answer that.

Recently, I witnessed a rather common display of a "one-size-fits-all" spiritual argument concerning rituals, or rather a blot, in an online group. What I observed was arrogance and attacking as one group's way of performing a blot was not the way another group performs their blot and there were some rather disturbing verbal slangs being thrown by both parties.

In all honesty, no one knows how the ancient ones performed their ceremonies, as no one living today was actually there to see with their own eyes an actual blot, if that's what they actually were called. There is no one-size-fits-all in an individual's practice and communication with the gods. I do not know of a single person on this planet that knows for sure the facts of the ancient past. Do you? What we have are knowledgeable people sharing their perspectives and viewpoints (just as I am doing) but none of them are experts!

Snorri Sturluson is given much credit for his writings but very few know that he was actually Christian. Who can say if his Christian background came into play in his writings? Not to mention the fact that his writings came about some couple of hundred years after the fact. We can appreciate his works as being his work, but our interpretation and implementation of them is again up to the individual. There is no room for a one-size-fits-all mentality. This only creates toxic boxes that impose conformity and feed patriarchy. As a public figure, I see silly arguments break out all the time concerning trivial things that really do not need to be argued about. Was the blot invigorating? Did everyone who participated gain something from the blot?

Why spend time belittling others for doing things differently within their group or kinship? Is it a kinship, fellowship, coven or tribe? Honestly who cares! Does it work for you, the individual? Is your group happy? If so then keep doing what you are doing!

Katie Gerrard writes in her book, *Seidr: the Gate is Open*, that: "There is no 'how-to' guide." The truth is that even groups who are apparently all using the same book have an enormous amount of differences within their practice. Each person on this planet is unique and an individual. When we circle together to raise energy in group ceremony or ritual, we are merging our individual energy with the individual energies of all those present in the hope of complimenting the intention or concept of the ceremony or ritual. It's a blending! Each person is just another ingredient to the stew, so to speak, and their energy will add or detract, but that's entirely up to their level of participation.

"Know before you go" is a good practice. Typically, groups leading rites or ceremonies are invite-only affairs with very little open to the public. Thought, planning, time and energy go into creating a ceremony and with that usually come directions or insights offered to those who are attending. Some groups prefer a more spontaneous ceremony, while others are much scripted and performed similar to a play that you would see on the stage. It should be okay to ask questions and seek council before attending, even if that is "what can I expect" or "how can I prepare?"

Each group also has their own code of conduct which is typically made known before joining. I have attended circles, for example, that refuse to even reference Loki in any way, shape or form while, myself, I lead ceremonies to intentionally invite Loki. We, as a society, need to stop expecting ourselves to show up in others and allow others to simply be themselves.

If you would like to move through already created rituals, blots and ceremonies then I strongly recommend that you seek out the ones found within the following books:

- *Essential Asatru – Walking the Path of Norse Paganism* by Diana L. Paxson.
- *The Way of Fire and Ice – the Living Tradition of Norse Paganism* by Ryan Smith.
- *Baldr's Magic – the Power of Norse Shamanism and Ecstatic Trance* by Nicholas E. Brink.
- *Norse Goddess Magic Trancework, Mythology and Ritual* by Alice Karlsdottir.
- *Seidr: the Gate is Open* by Katie Gerrard.

For those wanting to dive into the rites of shapeshifting and Berserker trance, I would recommend:

- *Werewolf Magick* by Denny Sargent, and also watch the movie, *The Northman*, which shows a full and, in my opinion, accurate rite of awakening the Berserker.

The following rituals and ceremonies are ones that have been created and performed by myself, both solitary and in group (which we call "wolf pack"). It should be noted that my training is anchored in Wicca and its practices do bleed into the rites and ceremonies. Please remember that your path is your own to define – if you wish to define it or categorize it in a specific tradition then that is yours and yours alone. No one has the right to dictate to you how you should communicate and call to the gods.

HAMMER RITE

This rite is adapted from numerous sources with the intent being to use Thor's Hammer "Mjolnir" as a tool to physically create, cast and establish ritual space. It has been compared to the ringing of the bell in other traditions. We have an antique hammer (which has been blessed and dedicated) that we use when dedicating space for ritual.

The hammer is held and each direction faced while the sign of the hammer is made. To perform the sign of the hammer, hold the hammer in your dominant hand, out in front of you with arm extended; move to the left, then to the right, then raise the hammer up and then down level to your heart. If you are performing this as a group, fellowship, grove, coven or pack then you can have attendees follow along using their hand extended. I find it helpful to explain the sign of the hammer to everyone attending the ritual.

To perform the sign of the hammer as a participant in group ritual, you will hold your dominant hand in front of you with arm extended, almost as if you are telling someone to stop; move your hand to the left of you, to the right, then raise your hand up and then down level to your heart. It does look like you are making the sign of the Christian cross. Please keep in mind that Christianity borrowed quite a few practices from the Pagans and this sign could very well have been one of them.

While turning to each direction, a summoning to Thor is expressed by the one holding the hammer.

Since we are working with Norse energies (people of the North), I start the Hammer Rite in the north:

"Hail Thor, with your hammer in the north,
Hallow and hold this sacred space – Hail Thor.
Hail Thor, with your hammer in the east,
Hallow and hold this sacred space – Hail Thor.
Hail Thor, with your hammer in the south,
Hallow and hold this sacred space – Hail Thor.
Hail Thor, with your hammer in the west,
Hallow and hold this sacred space – Hail Thor.
Hail Thor with your hammer in the earth,
Hallow and hold this sacred space – Hail Thor.
Hail Thor with your hammer in the sky,
Hallow and hold this sacred space – Hail Thor."

Once the space has been dedicated, I often pause, place the hammer on the center altar and then call to the god(s) or animals that are being welcomed to join this rite and then continue with the task, concept, intention and body of ritual. For example, if you are working with a specific rune to amplify healing or fertility within your group then it would be a good idea to call to Odin, sing or chant the specific rune and maybe even craft that rune as a group in a physical way.

When the rite is coming to its end, a simple way to open up the container or space is to offer gratitude to the god(s) or animals that were invited and then move back through the Hammer Rite. When I perform this, it is very much similar to casting a Wiccan circle. Holding the hammer up to the sky, recite:

> "Thor with your hammer in the sky, farewell.
> Thor with your hammer in the earth, farewell.
> Thor with your hammer in the west, farewell.
> Thor with your hammer in the south, farewell.
> Thor with your hammer in the east, farewell.
> Thor with your hammer in the north, farewell."

Raise your drinking horns or chalice and end with the toast "*Skal*". Sip your mead, wine or beer and the rite is complete. Good practice is to always pour out a little of the libations upon the earth or in a separate vessel for the gods.

CASTING A CIRCLE

There are many ways to create a protective barrier or cast a circle energetically for your ceremony or ritual. There are many tools one can implement as well. As a witch and practitioner of Seidr, my preference is to call upon the Dwarves found in Norse mythology (*Gylfaginning*, Prose Edda book) to assist me in guarding or warding the four cardinal points or directions.

Clear your space with sacred smoke, incense and then call to the Dwarves:

Nordri – north, Austri – east, Sudri – south, Vestri – west.

When I call upon the Dwarves, it is usually done in a chant; repeating their names over and over again until there is a shift in the energy. This is done in conjunction with the Hammer Rite, typically before the hammer is picked up and Thor called on to offer his protection. There is quite a bit of energy that raises when you have a group all chanting together.

SUMBEL

"Eat, drink and be merry" is a common term used in modern paganism. A Sumbel is just that! Lots of toasting with liquid libation. While mead or ale is the preferred libation; wine, water or tea is just as nice. Cater to your guests. During the month of December, when it's Yuletide, our community will often incorporate a Sumbel into our rite as a celebration of toasting, cheer and merriment. Each guest has their own chalice, drinking horn or cup that is filled with whatever liquid the individual desires. Moving in a circle, each guest toasts out loud a moment of celebration from their past year that created warmth and joy in their lives. After which, the entire group raises their cup, chalice or drinking horn and toasts with a loud boisterous *"Skal!"* (which means *"cheers!"*). Skal is a way of expressing goodwill and fortune.

Our community Yule event consists of a Hammer Rite and Sumbel, a summoning or call to Odin and Skadi and a gift-giving celebration. In our community, we are very much anchored into animism, so an animal relating to the season and intention of each ritual is always invited. Reindeer were and continue to be very sacred to the Sami people. These magnificent creatures are very much connected to Yuletide. This past Yule we anchored into reindeer energy with a call to the Reindeer Mother. The following are invocations that were used at our most recent ritual:

CALL TO ODIN

Allfather, Wise One.
He who sacrificed much for greater wisdom.
He who speaks in rhyme and riddles.
Old One, One-Eyed.
He who wanders.
He who is bringer of gifts.
He who welcomes the stillness of thought.
We welcome you. Hail Odin.

(Chant the "Fehu" rune)

CALL TO SKADI

Lady of Winter. Giantess!
Goddess of the Season.
Mother of Wolves.
She who tucks us in under her thick blanket of white.
She who wields the Isa rune urging us to be still, to freeze and push
    pause.
We welcome you. Hail Skadi.

(Chant the "Isa" rune)

CALL TO REINDEER MOTHER

Here in hallowed, sanctioned space we call to Reindeer Mother.
She whose antlers reach into the beyond as tethers to the other worlds.
She who is calm, serene and offers a gentle love.
We call to Reindeer Mother.
Fill this hearth and home with warmth, that all may survive this winter
    that is upon us.
Offer us your protection.
We call to Reindeer Mother.

She who is life giving, life sustaining.
She who is milk-giver.
She who brings back the Sun.
Offer us your magical flight, that we may celebrate the joy of new
    beginnings, that we may know the light will return.
We call to Reindeer Mother. Hail and welcome.

Our Sumbel consisted of three rounds of toasting. The first round honored Odin as each guest was asked to share or offer words of wisdom. The second round honored Skadi as each guest offered reminders of stillness. The third round honored Reindeer Mother as each guest offered motherly advice. Following the toasting, we enjoyed a festive gift exchange. Our rite ended with loud howling.

There are many ways to connect and physically reach out to the ancient gods. Some rituals and ceremonies are more elaborate than others and some are very spontaneous. In my backyard I have constructed a *harrow*, which is a pile of stones that have been mortared together with altar slabs in the base and near the top. This is where, in my solitary practice, I offer devotion. Each day I will go out, light incense, call to the Dwarves Nordri, Austri, Sudri and Vestri; chanting their names as I focus my energy on feeling them come forward to help me create a protective barrier. I will light a candle and call to Odin, Frigga and Freya, then I sit and allow myself to enter a trance-like meditative state. There is no set time or scripted-out ceremony; just me being fully present and anchored into my practice. Sometimes I will read, cast the runes or journey in meditation to have communication with the gods. When my rite is complete, I offer gratitude to Odin, Frigga, Freya and the Dwarves; then I pour over the top of the harrow a liquid libation to give tangible gratitude.

Wolves too have their own ceremonies and rituals. These are not questioned or criticized. As humans, we observe in reverence and awe when wolves howl to celebrate a good hunt or mourn a loved-one. We seem to respect animals preparing their dens in their own unique way. We don't redirect the wolf pack when they circle up, moving in one direction rather than the other and yet we rarely offer this same respectful energy to our fellow humans. We are often quick to correct, critique and attack solitary practitioners or groups for doing their ceremonies in ways that we do not. Why is this? Why are we investing so much time into sticking our heads into the business and practices of others? Let's offer them the same respect we do the wolves and allow individuals and groups to connect with their gods, however they choose.

CHAPTER THIRTEEN

Invoking Skadi

The dictionary defines "invoking" as: to call for with earnest desire, make supplication or pray for, to call on a deity or muse as in prayer or supplication, to declare to be binding or in effect. To "summon" means: to command the deity or god(s) to manifest or come to.

In my experience, I have observed and participated in both invoking and summoning. While some strongly advise against summoning, my caution would be to make sure you possess a basic understanding and have some kind of devotional relationship with the deity or god your are summoning before you demand they come to you. In my personal practice, my focus is on invoking rather than summoning. As a mere human, I can't imagine making demands on a god and then asking them for help or guidance, but that's just me.

Skadi is a force. Much like Thor; when her energy enters the room there is an energetic shift. With Thor I feel electricity, the hairs on my arm raise and there is an excitement in the air. With Skadi there is almost a sense of awe mixed with fear. The best way to describe it is to imagine being outside in a forest and all of a sudden a wolf pack appears and begins to circle you. Intense!

Welcoming Skadi into your life, solitary or group practice can be as intense as you want it to be. For some, she will bring a wildness to rituals and ceremonies; to others, she may become a matron that is honored and revered, called upon for years. To others still, she may simply be a mirror of strength and tenacity to call upon when one needs a reminder of one's own strength and tenacious attributes.

Working with any deity, again, should always be a personal quest to not only observe but to get to know the individual deity more intensely so that you can gain new perspectives and hopefully add to your life, practice and group.

Skadi, as an individual, mirrors complexity and polarities. As a goddess, she shows us that being loyal to one's kin is everything! To fight till the death to avenge her father's death and hold those responsible to account is admirable. We see very little loyalty in today's world of humankind.

As Wolf Mother and leader of the wolf pack modality, Skadi again offers us a gift so inspiring that people all over the world have honored, admired and worshipped her wolves as literal gods among men. Her wolves are the teachers and the masters. She provides us with these magnificent creatures to not only read about, study and observe, but to learn from by tangibly implementing their way of life into our own.

The most powerful and life-changing way to invoke any deity is to implement their attributes and teachings within our own lives on a daily basis. While working with gods or goddesses can be challenging; working with them in their animal aspect can be a bit easier. As humans, we can grasp things that we physically can see – and we can physically see wolves.

In my solitary and community efforts, implementing wolf pack modality has shifted every aspect of my life. Encouraging each individual to honor their inner wolf and to see that they each have a vital part to play within the pack can offer a heightened sense of awareness and responsibility. Holding others accountable is not easy but within a pack, if one wolf is lacking, the entire pack feels it.

Loyalty, honor and devotion are key components in invoking Skadi and her wolves into one's life and practice. It is sad but most people are lacking any real sense of loyalty. Honoring one's word is becoming a rare idea, rather than something that was fought for and upheld. Devotion to family, pack and one's practice is also becoming rare. Humans are super-quick to throw each other away, regardless of blood-ties or time spent formulating relationships. Social media has created an easy outlet for us to block, un-friend and toss away anyone, mostly out of pride, ego and resistance to constructive communication. When we implement wolf into our interactions, we can be reminded that communication is literally everything.

So, whether you invoke, invite, summon, command or offer devotion to Skadi as humble student, be sure to expect intensity and at times brutal truths as she is not one to tolerate half-assed dabbling. Skadi is one who is so confident and whole unto herself that those two attributes alone make her intimidating to connect with and reach out to, but those two attributes are often what draws people towards her. Who doesn't want more confidence? Who doesn't want to feel unabashedly whole unto themselves?

Be patient and be direct with your devotion. Are you looking to Skadi as goddess? Is she what you would consider or hope to consider as a matron deity? What does that level of devotion look like? For years I looked to and worked with the Celtic Goddess Brigid as my matron deity. I set an altar of devotion to her. I lit incense and candles daily while opening myself up as an empty vessel to be filled with her wisdom. Countless hours of meditation, reading, writing, chanting and singing were spent devoted to Brigid.

With age comes experience and now the thought of limiting myself to just one deity or the *need* of just one matron/patron feels off-balanced for me. Now I call to many gods/goddesses for specific counsel or rituals/ceremonies. While I still think of myself as a daughter of Brigid and tend her sacred flame, I am also one of Skadi's wolves, Odin's devotees and daughter of Gaia. I allow myself to be fluid and ride the waves of life, being competent in my knowledge of the many different deities out there. I have an arsenal of Ancient Ones to call upon as needed.

At times, I watch my students who are new to the Craft struggle with the concept of deity relationships, especially if they are recently healing from patriarchy and Christianity. The solution that always works is to take them back to a more animistic way of viewing life. While Skadi has incredible attributes and her saga is one to remember and learn from, it can still be uncomfortable for some to view her as a goddess to worship, answer to or offer devotion to. Embracing her aspect of wolves seems to create a more gentle and approachable relationship.

When honoring Skadi as wolves, there are many layers to consider. Do you see her as alpha wolf, leading the pack? We have learned that to lead the pack is really to lead from the back in a more protective and observant manner. As Mother of Wolves, can you see yourself as a wolf that is willing to work within the pack modality? Can you awaken the sleeping wolf, be a bit wilder and still work well with others for the survival of the whole rather than the self?

Skadi for me is both goddess and wolf, for I choose to not see a distinction that separates them from each other. Wolves are god-like. They are masters of teaching in ways that are simple if we only push pause, freeze and observe. Skadi is wild, free and knows when to seek isolation and when to charge into action. Her characteristics to me are god-like but not in an unobtainable way. When I really take time to look into the mirror, I can see all her attributes within myself. Maybe I do not always implement them in perfect timing but I possess them all.

The ability to observe life and breathe in the little things is a magic whole unto itself. There are times where I am a very busy wolf, going going going, near exhaustion when the Isa rune will appear and I am reminded to slow down, chill out and freeze for just a moment and just be present. It is Skadi that I offer gratitude to in moments like these.

The essence of Skadi is of *giantess* proportions. Working with her from the many standpoints of goddess, wolf and mirror has shifted my life's perspective in countless ways, beyond being able to describe. When I want more strength, she reminds me that I need to work hard, sacrifice much and keep going, even when I want to give up. When I am feeling overwhelmed, a quick cold shower reminds me to freeze for just a couple minutes and slow down, regroup and recharge.

As one who has worked with wolves as my primary spirit animal and totem for our community, Skadi as wolf has been the most amazing example of how to live with unique individuals and still thrive. Wolf has been and always will be my greatest teacher and life-shifting god. The wolf (like authentic human beings) is under attack, with humans being their most deadly predator. We are, through ego, pride and the need to conquer and compete, creating the death of humanity. There is no "thrive" if we continue to fight each other.

Wolves within the pack do not fight for elevation or status. They know that both are earned in due time, based on their involvement in the pack and its natural hierarchy. Wolves do not strategize on how to take out the mama and papa wolf, yet we see this in humans all the time. The ones who have put in the most work, time and effort – we see them as the ones who need to go. What a weird concept? Why can't we just be happy where we are and allow those who have achieved much to be celebrated for their accomplishments? Why do we have to hunt them down? Why do we have to see each other as predators? Why do we see those who are weaker than us or less accomplished than us as our prey?

Humanity has a sickness, one that we all feed in one way or another. We fight for survival in a world where were no one is going to survive, it's fascinating. What if we supported, encouraged and allowed everyone their own authentic growth without forcing obligations, expectations and demands on how they grow? I love the quote: "A flower does not think of competing with the flower next to it – it just blooms." Wolves do not waste time making silly comparisons with each other. The bear does not spend countless hours observing (scrolling) on the nearby raven's life to covet or make comparisons. The bear just goes on being a bear and the raven goes on being a raven – both accepting of each other.

When I invoke Skadi, it is often to help me remember that everyone I meet is just a different kind of wolf. We are all part of the same wolf pack that is called humanity and we all need each other in one way or another in order to survive. So let's all start acting like we are part of the same pack. Skadi as Mother of Wolves I believe would want every wolf in the pack to survive and thrive. So let's do that! Let's honor her legacy by living our most bold, confident, wild and authentic lives. Let's allow the other wolves in our life to do the same and see how our human pack shifts and transforms into one unstoppable force.

SKADI

Mother of Wolves.
She who protects each individual within the pack.
Goddess of Winter,
who reminds us there is a season to slow down, pause and reset.
Great Giantess. Fierce Lady.
We call to you. We welcome you.
She who is bold, confident, loyal and brave,
remind us that we too are capable of all things.
We too have those in our lives that support us.
We too can be of support in return.
Queen of the Mountain. Wolf Woman.
Hear our howling hearts cry as we call to you.
Hail Skadi.

Wolf Pack of Ice Queens

For the past two decades, my life has been anchored into goddess spirituality. Through this journey, I have made attempts to learn, call upon and share many different goddess activation workshops with my community. Here is a compilation, a gathering of goddesses who fit into the *Ice Queen* category. This wolf pack is perfect for those who are wanting to offer group sessions or simply want to create a personal connection with specific deities or who want to activate within themselves the attributes they share when looking at each Ice Queen as mirror.

LILITH

Her many names and titles: Queen of the Night, Mother of Demons, first wife of Adam. She is a Sumerian goddess linked to the Temple of Inanna. Once known as the Mother Goddess herself, she is the first true liberator. She was also known as a hag, screecher, vampire and succubus. The first feminist goddess! Her name means "screech owl" or "night creature".

She encourages all women to stand up for what they believe – to be unbridled, no matter the cost. She encourages all women to seek equality, to be brave!

Lilith stands for freedom, courage, playfulness, passion, pleasure and sexuality. Lilith is a dangerously beautiful goddess who refused to be a subordinate to Adam. She believed herself to be his equal. Lilith was turned away from paradise for her "crime" and has been depicted in artwork as a demon. She is also portrayed as having both the wings and claws of a bird. Some have painted her as part-snake.

- **To internalize Lilith's fairness, bravery and exuberant lustiness – eat an apple. Quite literally, take a bite out of life.**

Sacred symbols of Lilith: apple and snake.
Stones: amber, tiger's eye, garnet, bloodstone, tourmaline, smoky quartz.
Mantra: equality.
Scents: ylang-ylang, black pepper, bitter orange, rosewood, lemongrass, eucalyptus, bergamot and peppermint

Suggested affirmations:
I forgive, I welcome forgiveness, I am free from judgment, I deserve to be free from guilt, I am creating the life I love, I am honest and truthful in all I say and do, I am in charge of my body and my sexuality.

"I DANCE MY LIFE FOR MYSELF"

Lilith Fair was a concert tour and music festival founded by Sarah McLachlan. This festival took place during 1997–1999. It consisted solely of female artists and female-led bands. McLachlan started the festival because she was outraged by the sexual discrimination that venues displayed towards female artists.

DISCOVER YOUR DARK AND WILD SIDE

"You're either a goddess or a doormat."

– Pablo Picasso.

Being nice is not always a virtue. Playing the good girl and acting sweet all the time does not always get you what you want in life. If you want to really live your life true to you then you have to be able to take some risks, let your hair down, be bold, dare to push buttons, be a bit provocative. You have to be prepared to break some hearts, hurt some feelings and demand what you want.

Invoke Lilith when you are ready to break free – when you truly want to unleash your wild woman, when you have had enough of oppression and are ready to take control of your life, regardless of the consequences, regardless of who may choose to be offended along the way. It is your life – "take no shit" and "bow down to no one!"

WAYS TO HARNESS HER WILD, UNLEASHED, FIERCE ENERGY

1. Watch movies that celebrate Lilith's wildness – she's a bit nasty with a whole shit-load of bad-ass attitude. She knows what she wants and she gets it.
   (What are some movies featuring a leading lady with this type of attitude?)
2. Practice being fierce – you have got to start saying "NO" when you mean it. Stop making compromises. Stop doing things to make others uncomfortable. Lilith doesn't give a fuck if other people are comfortable. She lives her life for her and no one else.
   (Write down how many times you say you're sorry in one day.)
3. Get out your whips and chains! Put on some black leather and spiked heels and be the dominatrix of your life! No one argues with a "DOM."

4. Don't blame other people for you not having the life you want – if you are a parent, don't blame your spouse or your children – you chose to marry and have kids. If you are employed, don't blame your boss, you wanted the job. Don't blame your parents – they have done the best they could. OWN YOUR SHIT!!!!!! OWN YOUR SHIT!!!!!! If you are disappointed, angry or irritated – own it. You chose each of those emotions. No one – let me repeat – NO ONE can *make* you feel anything!

LILITH: QUEEN OF THE NIGHT

First feminist goddess, dating back to 2300 BCE or earlier.

Her many names: Mother of Demons, first wife of Adam, Sumerian succubus, Handmaid of Inanna, Mother Goddess, female tiger, wisdom principle, ultimate feminine bad-ass bitch, Goddess of Liberation, the Dark Maid, Maiden of Desolation, the first woman created, Night Demon or Demoness.
Gemstones: amber, tiger's eye, garnet, bloodstone, tourmaline and smoky quartz.
Mantra: EQUALITY!!!!!
Chakra: solar plexus/power chakra (rules personal power, metabolism and intuition).
Attributes: wisdom, playfulness, freedom, courage, passion and sexuality.
Essential oils: lemongrass, eucalyptus, rosewood, peppermint, bergamot, lime, lemon and myrtle (restore, stimulate, promote clarity, assertiveness and confidence).
Animals: snakes and owls.
Objective: when working with Lilith, be prepared – she is a dark goddess for a reason. Her job is to help you dig up old flaws and throw them in your face. She wants to help you push your boundaries and send you on a trial-by-fire, if you are ready for that.

Ways to activate her:
1. Talk to her regularly.
2. Make offerings – red wines, dancing and sex.
3. Listen to your gut – if you want to hear her, she will make you listen. Chances are that you will feel it first in your gut – your place of instincts.

Why activate her?
1. If you need to leave an abusive relationships (protection).
2. If you need more self-confidence (conquer fear).
3. To enhance your sex life – magical sexual work.

She is that fighting spirit in all women that makes them fight for their own causes and the causes of others. Lilith is the renegade!

Question & answer segment:
- Do you really think Lilith is a demon?
- Or was she demonized because she spoke out against "God" and his law of marriage?
- Why do you feel that you need Lilith in your life? How can she help you?

Dark Goddess defined:
The Dark Goddess is represented by the New Moon. She is the Crone. She is both the cradle and the grave. She is a warrior, a protector and a wise-woman.

> "Come to me at the Dark Moon and see that which can not be seen, face the shadow that is yours alone."

A WORD OF CAUTION BEFORE YOU MOVE FORWARD IN INVOKING LILITH.

Remember that she is considered a "dark goddess" which means she will activate and awaken your dark side – your shadow self. She takes no shit and she demands that you give none. If you ask her to help you with something, be prepared to see that through to the end. She will give you strength and courage, even help you to activate that inner bitch that you suppress so often but you, my dear, have to do the work.

It's up to you to own that when you embrace her energy, people are not going to like you. People are going to get offended. People are going to have some hurt feelings. You need to own that. You need to acknowledge the role you choose and play it. Lilith will remind you. She will keep you on your toes and it might not be pleasant at times. She may awaken things in you that at the time you will feel unprepared to accept. You may even be a bit afraid. She is not going to care. You called her in – so deal with the outcome.

She was known as a demon for a reason. At times, she may feel very demonic. Grow up! You called her in. You asked for it. You invited her.

Lilith is bold. She is probably, next to Kali, the most in-your-face bitch goddess that you will work with and, believe me; you will know when she has been invited to your party because she will stay until she is ready to leave. She will cause some chaos; stir up things you thought you could hide. She will bring to the surface all your insecurities, which you will have to own and address. You are really going to do some shadow work with this powerhouse. Are you ready?

INVOKING LILITH ENERGY

Let's begin with our breath.
Take a nice deep cleansing breath in … and now exhale it out …

(Repeat 3 times)

Now breathe in … 2 … 3 … 4 … and out … 2 … 3 … 4 …

(Repeat 3 times)

Now breathing at your own pace, breathe fully and breathe easily.

Using your imagination, I want you to picture yourself on a nice warm sunny beach. See yourself relaxing, soaking up the heat of the Sun's rays on your skin. This is where your conscious mind will rest while we activate the subconscious and go on a journey.

Taking another deep breath in, you are ready to take your subconscious on this journey. See yourself moving forward through a jungle. The trees and foliage are thick and it's hard to see more than twenty feet ahead of you. There are many obstacles in your way; large boulders, fallen trees and the thick foliage make it difficult to make much progress – but you are determined. Moving through this jungle, it is natural to feel a bit uneasy, frustrated and even angry, especially as the trees, boulders and foliage create an even thicker obstacle. In this state, you may feel like you want to scream or cry. Allow the feelings to surface. Give yourself permission to embrace these so-called negative emotions. Feel them – feel the frustration, the irritation, the anger. In this state, you collapse onto your knees and are almost ready to quit.

Then you hear laughter in the jungle. You turn to follow the sound and you see a woman. This woman is naked – she stands very straight and tall. You see at her feet hundreds of snakes slithering about. Draped over her shoulder is a much larger snake. She is laughing at you – a deep, husky from-the-belly laugh. She finds your frustration and irritation funny.

You begin to get upset, almost angry at her. She doesn't care. She stands there and just laughs. Your frustration level may be hitting a peak. You may feel outraged that she is being so rude. Suddenly she stops laughing and jumps down from where she is standing. She slowly yet with a fierce determination moves towards you, her movement graceful, almost snake-like. She is beyond intimidating. Don't look this goddess in the eye – not yet. In fact, you begin to look down, or away – anything to avoid eye contact. She doesn't care, she keeps moving forward, until she is standing right in front of you.

She softly lifts your chin with her calloused hand and demands that you look at her. She speaks and her voice is as husky and deep as her laugh: "I am Lilith – you have come to my jungle to overcome obstacles. How can you do that when your emotions cloud your judgment? Had you come to this jungle with confidence and some fierceness then you would have seen the fallen trees as simply twigs, the boulders as mere pebbles and the thick foliage as minute weeds. For you see, in life there are going to be many road blocks, obstacles and debris standing in your way. That is for certain. You cannot control everything, but you can conquer each one by simply changing your perspective and, most importantly, your attitude. Are you ready? Are you strong enough? Or are you going to be defeated? Remember, you won't be defeated by life or what it throws your way – it is your weaknesses, doubts and fears that will defeat you. They will crush you. You will crush you. You are your biggest obstacle. You are the one standing in your way."

Lilith's words ring true. Even though she is scolding you in an angry, vicious tone, you know she is right. When you are ready and ONLY if you are ready, ask Lilith what you want her help with.

If you are not ready or do not have anything to ask her help with then give her thanks for her time and see yourself leaving the jungle, returning to your beach.

However, if you do have something you are ready to ask her help with – maybe it's to have more confidence, more passion or simply more fierceness – then ask her, ever so nicely.

Lilith listens to your requests and says: "Are you sure?" If you are certain, then nod your head. Lilith cautions you to be careful in what you ask for. She chuckles a little and pulls you in for a hug. She squeezes you tight and gives you a kiss on the cheek. As she pulls away, she gives you a little smirk and winks. Before she leaves, she places both hands on your face and kisses you fully on the mouth – a soft, warm and passionate kiss. She laughs as she walks away from you, her snakes slithering on the ground beneath her. She turns one last time and tosses you an apple. She says: "Take a bite." With this, she really laughs – that deep, husky, belly laugh.

You look hesitantly at the apple in your hand and figure "what the hell" – you asked and she gave. You sink your teeth into the sweetest apple you have ever tasted. You know that this apple is a sacred symbol of divine wisdom. When you bite into this apple you are taking in this divine wisdom – the knowledge that you are divine. Lilith may be fierce and intimidating but she is just showing you a part of yourself that you may keep hidden. With this apple she reminds you that, once again, all the power is yours. Stop battling with yourself and making your life harder than it needs to be. Own your shit! Accept your shit! And, most importantly, bow down to no one!!!

As you leave the once overgrown jungle, you enjoy every bite of your apple and you feel invigorated and energized. You chuckle to yourself at the thought of how frustrated and intimidated you were at the beginning of this journey. Each step now feels effortless.

Take a nice deep breath and see yourself back on the beach. Feel once again the Sun on your skin. With all this new confidence and energy, there is nothing standing in your way – you can create your life exactly how you want it to be. Now you just want to celebrate.

See yourself shedding your clothes (if you have any on) and running down the beach into the ocean. Feel the water crash against you as you swim out past the break and just float. Feel how truly weightless you are and how free. Let the ocean wash away any residual doubts or fears. When you are ready, throw back your head and just laugh!

Now slowly begin to take notice of your surroundings. Feel your feet and hands beginning to move. Feel yourself slowly coming back to the present – invigorated and ready!

THE GODDESS BASTET

Bast, Bastet or Basthet:
Egyptian Goddess of Sensuality, protector of the home and health-bringer. Also known as the Cat Goddess. Daughter of the Sun God Ra. She is known as the Lady of the East, Goddess of the Rising Sun and the Sacred and All-seeing Eye. She is also considered a Moon Goddess and Goddess of Music and Dance. Bast was also associated with fertility and childbirth. She is known as the sister to the Goddess of Destruction – Sekhmet. The ancient Greeks referred to Bastet as the Egyptian Artemis.

Her story:
It is said that by day she walked as a woman and at night she transformed into a cat (known for their keen night-vision). Because of her all-seeing sacred eye, called the Utchat, she was able to see magically in the dark, making her Goddess of the Moon. She is depicted as a slender woman with the head of a cat. She was worshiped around 3500 BC. Her shrine is in Baubastis. Fashioned from blocks of pink granite and lined with enormous trees, her temple was considered to be one of the most beautiful temples in the world. Cats were honored in her temple. Any cat that died would be restored to life by the Goddess Bastet. This

is possibly the source of the idea of cats having nine lives. Most houses displayed a small statue of Bast as a form of protection. Owning a cat was a way of inviting the goddess's protective energy into the home.

Her celebrations:
Many festivals and celebrations were held in her honor and were very similar in nature to our modern-day Mardi Gras – lots of dancing, frolicking and drinking. She was known to be the lover of EVERY god and goddess, making her the Goddess of Sensuality, Sex and Pleasure.

What she teaches:
Relax, never waste precious energy on negative things, enjoy all the beauty and taste life fully. Accept the true nature of things, including your truth. Play, frolic, fuck and celebrate!

She was known to some as the personification of the soul of Isis. She is the Lady of the East and her counterpart sister is Sekhmet, known as Lady of the West. She seemed to possess dual personalities – tame and feral.

In ancient history, she was first depicted as having the head of a lioness, similar to her sister. Later she was depicted as having the head of a domestic cat. This displays her dual personalities – or balanced personalities. She showed both a dark and light side. She did not have a mother because Ra, her father, was known as the Great He-She. In other legends, she was said to have been worshipped in northern Egypt, making her "She of the North," while Sekhmet was worshipped in southern Egypt, making Sekhmet "She of the South." With her head as a lion, she is the Sun Goddess; when her head is that of a cat, she is the Moon Goddess.

Bast:
Mother of all cats, she is a deity of fertility, motherhood, sexuality, love and music. In some stories she is said to be daughter of Ra

and Isis, while others say she was the firstborn daughter of Amun. She was married to Ptah. Bast has a gentle, loving disposition, but she is fiercely protective of her children. She does have a darker side.

Making a witch-cat jar:
A witch jar is designed to pull in any negativity that may be floating around the home. You can use glass marbles or polished stones to create a trap for the negative energy. Add some cat hair for protection and some catnip to enhance feline energy. Take a bay leaf and write on it the protection you are seeking. Place all ingredients in your jar and have your cat bless and sniff the jar to amp up the power. Call upon Bastet to bless and protect your home and invoke her energy into your cats, making them guardians.

Bastet Activation Tools
Stones: tiger's eye, sunstone, cat's eye.
Herbs: catnip and cinnamon.
Libations: milk, catnip
Incense: musk, cinnamon, myrrh, hemp and sandalwood.
Planet: Sun
Colors: green, gold and red.
Call upon her for: protection, more passion and play.
Animal: CATS!!!

Ways to activate her energy into your lives:
Dance, move like a cat, pet a cat, laugh, seduce yourself.

What she encourages:
Stop compromising, get rid of toxic people in your lives, don't let anyone or anything hold you down, you are a force of power and pleasure – start living it!

Bastet is Goddess of Celebration. She wants you to show both your light and your dark sides, your sexy side and your innocence. She is a goddess of duality. Most importantly – she is not ashamed. Be fierce when you need to be. Be sweet when you need to be. YOU CAN BE BOTH!!!!!!! Celebrate your independent nature – "Your independence is a foundation for your strength and success." Stop apologizing. Call on her to help with fertility issues, pregnancy and to enhance your sexuality.

MEDITATION TO CONNECT AND ACTIVATE BASTET

Sitting in a nice comfortable position, focusing on your breath, allow your mind to clear itself of outside thoughts, stresses and just let go.

Focusing on your breathing, take a nice inhale and exhale it out.

(Repeat 3 times)

In your mind's eye, I want you to see yourself in Egypt. Stand and get yourself centered.

Feel the heat of the desert sand underneath your feet, feel the heat of the Sun on your skin.

Breathe in deeply and really allow yourself to breathe in Egypt. There is magick in the air and you can feel it and taste it with each inhale. You have been here before and your surroundings feel very familiar. As you become more centered and anchored here in the desert, you begin to look around and notice that you are standing outside of Bastet's temple. Her temple is made of pink granite and the outside corridor is lined with numerous trees, creating an oasis. There are hundreds of cats strolling along and you begin to move closer to the entrance, seeking a quick glance of the goddess.

As you step closer, you get distracted by so many things along the way – there are so many flowers to stop and admire, there are so many cats to pet and play with. Soon you forget where you were going in the first place. It is so delightful to sit on the grass and enjoy the warmth of the Sun while kittens run along and pounce and play. You decide to just stay right where you are and just enjoy the little things for a moment or two. What can it hurt?

Time goes by as you relax in the moment but in the distance you hear a celebration going on.

You can hear laughter, music and singing. That sounds very enticing, so you decide to saunter towards the festivities.

As you approach, you can see the large granite doors to the entrance of the temple are open and inside there is quite the decadent celebration. The dancing is provocative and sexual. There is wine flowing freely and the music is intoxicating. You decide to partake.

As you dance and drink you see a figure tall and slender movingly through the crowd. A woman dark skinned with the head of a cat saunters and prowls, moving towards you. Along the way she stops to greet her guests, kissing them on the mouth, sipping their drinks, laughing – she herself is intoxicating.

She needs no introduction – everyone knows who this goddess is. This is her temple and you are participating in one of her infamous festivities. As she slowly and gracefully approaches you, there may be some feelings of excitement fluttering in your belly. She is quite stunning, standing before you completely nude, except for her jewelry. She reaches her hand out to meet yours and you stand there hand in hand for a few moments. She leans her face closer to yours and speaks in almost a purr – you can feel her black fur soft against your cheek. She whispers words only you can hear. Her message is unique as you are unique. She feels no need to speak out loud or address the group, you will hear her or you won't.

(Pause)

After she speaks to you, she moves in even closer and nuzzles your neck, sending a tingle down your spine. She breathes into your skin as her whiskers tickle your cheek. She kisses you softly and motions for you to follow. As you follow behind her, you notice how elegantly she moves, her gestures are almost cat-like. She stops suddenly and points to a large chaise lounge covered in thick furs. She motions for you to lay on it and make yourself comfortable. As you approach the chaise lounge, you strip down to nothing.

You lay on the chair with grace and the fur is so soft you can't help but stretch and rub your body against it. Bastet laughs in almost a purr and offers you a glass of wine – she wants you to indulge. She wants you to frolic and play. She wants you to remember to take time to enjoy the little things, to laugh more – to live more!!! Bastet leans down and looks into your eyes with her gold cat eyes. She tells you in her purr-like voice to: "Stop worrying so much, life is full of pleasure and sweetness. Open up and taste it, let go of things that weigh you down, rid yourself of people who hold you back; you need to celebrate more, play more and do more!!! Do more for you because you are worthy, but you don't really need me to tell you that."

With that she gets up and is lost in the crowd. You could follow if you wanted but there is no point and this chaise lounge is too decadent to leave. So you stay sprawled out, your body caressing the fur, sipping on your wine as you enjoy the dancing and merriment. You know her words to be true. She didn't need to tell you.

Take a slow deep breath in and let it all out. As you begin to focus on your breathing once more, you begin to become more aware of your surroundings.

PELE

Pele's many names: Goddess of Fire, she who shapes the sacred land. A very passionate and volatile force of destruction. Goddess of Lightening, Wind and Volcanoes. Madame Pele or Tutu Pele is a sign of respect. Pele of the Sacred Land.

One of her many legends: Pele was born of the Mother Goddess Haumea. Her father was the Sky God Wakea. Legend has it that Pele fled Tahiti (where she was born) and sought refuge in Hawaii – she fled because of her angry older sister who wanted to kill Pele because Pele had seduced her husband.

Pele's younger sister Laka is Goddess of Hula and the patroness of dance. Pele had many lovers who unfortunately did not survive her passionate temper and her fiery flames.

Pele has destroyed more than 100 structures on the Big Island since 1983 and, perhaps even more awesome than that, she has added more than 70 acres of land to the island's southeastern coastline. She is much respected.

Another legend: Pele, being a fire goddess, has many many lovers; she was quite a passionate lover. However, she was difficult, as any woman can be. It is said that the lava fields around Mauna Loa are filled with lava pillars – these pillars are the scorched remains of the lovers that displeased her. Hell hath no fury like a woman scorned (a woman who has been rejected by a man can be ferociously angry and vindictive).

Pele's story reminds us that when we know who we are and when we honor that energy, when we honor our true self, we will find our place in the world. We are also reminded, when we are pursuing our true path, to persevere despite perceived and self-created obstacles. We are encouraged to not give up just before we reach the destination of our dreams.

Pele is ruler of the volcanoes of Hawaii, and humans have no power to resist her. When Pele speaks, her words are final. She may appear as a tall, beautiful, young woman or as an old woman – a crone bent with age, sometimes accompanied by a white dog. There have been numerous accounts of passersby picking up a woman and a dog walking alongside the road, only to glance in their rear-view mirror and she has completely disappeared. Other stories tell of her appearing in photographs where there was no such woman physically present when the photo was taken.

When Pele is angry, she may appear as a woman engulfed in flames or as a pure flame. Her sacred spirit name is Ka-ula-o-ke-ahi, meaning "the redness of the fire."

Pele's gemstone: peridot – Hawaiian myth claims that these stones are her tears. Pele lives inside the largest active volcano in Hawaii, it is said that with every eruption Pele is expressing her longing to be with her true love. However, because of her fiery temperament, she is considered fickle, dangerous and short-tempered. Peridot is considered a good luck stone; it will attract abundance and love (lava rock and obsidian are stones that will show honor to Pele).

Pele essential scents: ginger, cinnamon, anise, lemon and basil.

Pele plants: ohelo are fruits related to blueberries and cranberries. It is customary to toss a berry in the direction of Kilauea (Pele's volcano) in honor to the goddess.

Pele's element: fire.

Pele's color: red.

Libations: coins, strawberries, hair, sugarcane, tobacco and brandy.

Her message: the spirit of Pele lives in each of us. Keep your temper in check. Recognize what upsets you and remember to pause before reacting. Stay calm. One can be both calm and fierce. She will help you to find your inner truth and purpose in your life, awakening your inner flame, passion and empowerment.

Pele's desire: unity, tradition, protection, creativity and change. She is the creative force that comes into our lives; cleansing, transforming, rebuilding – she is summer's fiery energy and flame.

Pele's attributes: beautiful, romantic, creative, feminine, powerful, proud, merciful, impulsive, active, spontaneous, giving, sexy, strong, simple, graceful, moody, emotional, hot, a doer, a lover, eruptive!

Power of fire: the element of fire brings energy – physical energy, motivation, empowerment and strength. Fire is useful for manifesting, purifying and igniting our souls. Fire has the power to transmute and clear old, stagnant energy. Fire can be invoked for protection – physically and energetically.

Call upon Pele when: you are feeling fatigued or burned out. She will help you to ignite your inner divine flames – refueling you and re-energizing your mind, body and spirit. She will help you to avoid burning the candle at both ends. She will remind you that rest and self care are vital to the refueling process.

Pele sets fire to the falsehoods that women are weak and incapable and that to be feminine means to be fragile and helpless. Pele shows us strength and power. She has literally destroyed and rebuilt an island, repeatedly. Pele loves and lives with profound passion, providing us with a platform for both women and men to transcend.

She helps us to be honest in our communication and to set boundaries. Pele brings confidence and courage and promotes positive action. Pele helps us to clear the illusions that we hide behind. She shows us our true potential.

Pele is dedicated to our true power, the power of divine love, she is devoted to helping us to realize and express our creative power in a way that brings benefit, blessings and beauty to the whole.

Through honoring our own inner fire and by realizing our innate and eternal connection to the divine energy, we will naturally feel alive with vital, vibrant energy and be naturally enthusiastic and empowered.

How to invite Pele into your life: anger and fire go hand-in-hand. When we direct anger at others, our words can burn and cause them pain. If we are on the receiving end of someone's anger then we are the ones that feel the burn and pain. Words of anger can destroy, just like fire, yet words of anger not expressed and instead suppressed can create internal emotional, physical and spiritual damage. We can offer our anger to Pele so we can learn to utilize it, channel it and heal its consequences in our lives.

1. Know yourself – what pushes your buttons?

Pele, Goddess of the Fiery Volcano, Lady of Light ......
I give to you my anger at _____.
I give to you my fear of _____.
I give to you whatever keeps me angry.
I give to you whatever keeps me from expressing how I feel.

End by telling Pele "mahalo" – which means "thank you" in Hawaiian.
Peace affirmation: Pele, Queen of Molten Lave, this is too hot for me to handle. I surrender this to you.

2. Manage your emotions:

Remember that you only have control over your emotions. No one has the power to *make* you feel anything. You choose anger and you embrace wrath. Own it, understand it and don't let it control you. Get a grip! Remember to push pause before you react.

3. Release your pent-up anger:

"Holding onto anger is like drinking poison and expecting the other person to die." Go to the gym, take a hike, hit some pillows, do scream therapy or, better yet, dance therapy.

PELE ACTIVATION MEDITATION

Let's begin by taking a nice deep breath in and letting it all out. Closing your eyes and focusing on your breath, allow yourself to clear your mind of outside thoughts and distractions, with each exhale blowing them away. Creating a blank, quiet space in your mind, breathe in 2-3-4 and out 2-3-4.

(Repeat 3 times)

Now that you are relaxed, use your imagination and see yourself standing on the beaches of Hawaii. Feel the sand under your feet as the water from the waves slowly caresses them. Smell the salty air of the ocean and really give yourself permission to breathe in the island. Standing here on the beach, you see a large mountain to your left. You notice a sandy path that leads to the very top. You decide to follow the path. Heading up to the top of the mountain, you can see the ocean below you and you can hear the waves crashing against the rocks, but you keep going.

Once you reach the top, the landscape is quite different. There are large lava stones and you realize that this mountain is actually the top of a volcano. You have heard stories of this volcano and you know it to be the Goddess Pele's volcano. Or is *she* the volcano?

Give yourself permission to walk right to the edge of the crater of the volcano, you can feel the heat in the air, and the ground as you approach is warm underneath your feet, but you are not afraid.

As you peer over the edge, you can see some smoke rising and you may even see a hint of a flame. Take a few deep breaths here and really allow yourself to connect with the power of Nature.

As you stand here, you see flames beginning to grow and a form is appearing from the center of the volcano – a woman is emerging from the flaming hot lava. She is beautiful, dark-skinned with soft brown eyes. She is both woman and flame, yet she is not fierce or unnerving in presence, instead she is very calm and soothing – at one with the fire, yet soft and delicate like a flower.

You know Pele to be a very passionate, fierce goddess of destruction, but she is also very gentle, protective and nurturing. She wants to help you clear out and destroy your insecurities, your anger and your pain.

Give yourself permission to move even closer to the edge. She is reaching out her hand to you. She is giving you permission to throw all your doubts, fears and angers into her volcano, her melting lava. When you are ready, see yourself releasing!! You may scream out your fears, toss in your anger, toss in your insecurities. There is no wrong way to release and let go. Just see yourself shedding them from you and allowing them to burn up in her lava. See the flames swallowing and melting them one by one. (Pause)

Once you have released and fed the volcano, Pele emerges from the flames and joins you. Standing right next to you, she is in full female form. She wraps her arms around you and you can feel her warmth. She soaks up any remaining seeds of anger and assures you that she will always be here for you when you need her. She urges you to not be controlled by your anger, insecurities or fears.

She tells you that she will help you to release them.

You feel so much relief and peace. You offer the goddess gratitude and libations in the form of a beautiful Hawaiian flower. She places her hand on your cheek and steps back into the center of the volcano.

As you move back towards the sandy path that led you here to the core of her power, you feel weightless and light-hearted with not a care in the world. You feel more confident and assured that you can take control of the situations and people who tend to get under your skin. You know that at any time you can return to her sacred mountain and give you anger, frustrations and insecurities to Pele.

As you reach the beach once again, you feel the splash of the ocean on your feet. Taking a nice deep breath here, you breathe in the salty air and you feel cleansed and rejuvenated – whole!

With each breath you take, you are beginning to become more and more aware of your surroundings – your feet beginning to move and your hands beginning to move, bringing you back to the present. Complete.

ATHENA

Athena: Greek Goddess of Wisdom and Crafts, known to the Romans as Minerva. Virgin Goddess – dedicated to chastity and celibacy. Beautiful, warrior, protector of chosen heroes and of Athens. She was the ONLY Olympian goddess portrayed wearing armor. She was protector of cities, patroness of military forces, Goddess of Weavers, Goldsmiths, Potters and Dressmakers. She was credited for creating the bridle to tame horses, inspiring ship builders and teaching people how to plow and rake. Goddess of Reason.

Her sacred plants: olives – the olive tree was her special gift to Athens.

Her sacred animal: owls – wisdom; snakes – rejuvenation.

Her sacred scent: patchouli, lemongrass, cedar and orange water.

Her sacred gemstone: lapis lazuli, onyx, ruby, turquoise and gold.

Her libations: wine, honey, olive oil, olives and bread.

Her colors: gold and orange.

Athena's myth or legend: Athena had a very dramatic entrance. Born of Zeus, she was a motherless daughter. She never knew her mother and was not born from the womb. Athena burst forth from Zeus' head. The story is that Zeus, of course, had many lovers and when Metis became pregnant with Athena, Zeus tricked her into becoming a small fly and he swallowed her, taking on her attributes and the baby she was carrying. Zeus had a horrific headache and he called upon Hephaistos the smith to break open his skull with an axe – with one swing. Athena leapt from the head of Zeus in full armor, letting out a wild battle cry. Athena considered herself born of one parent. She was her father's favorite. She was the ONLY one in Olympia that Zeus trusted – he even trusted her enough to let her be the ONLY one to ever hold his thunderbolt (his symbol of power).

Athena and Arachne: Athena, known for her power as Goddess of Weaving, was challenged by another weaver – Arachne. However, Arachne had decided to weave an image of Zeus' shortcomings. Athena humiliated Arachne, causing Arachne to hang herself. However, Athena was not satisfied, so she transformed Arachne into a spider – forever to be condemned to hang by a thread and spin. Thus spiders are known as arachnids. Athena and the patriarchy: a virgin goddess, she never married and never wanted to. She was, however, a protector, advisor and ally of many heroes.

- Perseus was able to defeat the Medusa with the help of Athena, who taught him to utilize mirrors to avoid her Medusa's gaze, thus enabling him to kill her and avoid being turned to stone.
- Jason and the Argonauts were helped by Athena, who built their ship which allowed them to capture the Golden Fleece.
- Bellerophon was given a golden bridle by Athena, which allowed him to capture and tame the winged horse Pegasus, which came to the aid of Hercules during his twelve tasks.
- Achilles was watched over by Athena.
- Odysseus was given aid and protection on his long journey home by Athena.

Athena was the best strategist during the Trojan War.

She sided with patriarchy, stating that patriarchy ranked principle above maternal bonds.

Why do you think she did that?

Athena was not born of a woman; she was not raised by a mother. She was born a warrior in full armor – she was more masculine-dominated in her traits. Athena strives in business, academic, scientific, military and political arenas.

Which women in the public eye today can you think of that display Athena-like attributes?

As Goddess of Wisdom, she is more logical – ruled by her head, not her heart. She is very tactical in her thought process. In the midst of an emotional storm, Athena will be rational and find her bearings before reacting. She is very practical and logical.

In which ways are you like Athena?

Can you name some careers today that would fit women with more of Athena's mindset or attributes?
Her attributes: extrovert, practical, intelligent, loyal, inspiring, independent, brilliant, tireless, courageous, successful and an achiever. Athena loves a good dare.

Athena is concerned with the ways of the world:

Unlike Artemis, who wanted to escape and be in the wild, Athena wants to be right in the middle of the hustle and bustle. She loves the arena of political debates, the business of the market. The rebirth of Athena can be seen right now – in today's presidential candidates.

Athena, full armored, wants to be in the thick of things. The heat of the battle does not intimidate her. She herself is a feminist heroine. To be an Athenian woman means to be tough. Thus, she was born fully armored. In order to do her job and get women to rise up and not rely on men so much, she had to be the leading example. Athenian women today, like any oppressed minority, have to be twice as good as the guardians of the structure against which they must prove themselves, whatever the arena of endeavor.

Her armor: is a metaphor that psychologically describes a well defended ego. She does not have to be defensive, she is aggressively self-confident. This is the warrior goddess emerging.

In which ways are you armored? In what circumstances are you or have you displayed aggressive self-confidence? Defensiveness?

Finding balance: how can one achieve balance? Is Athena balanced? Why? Give examples.

For three years I wore the armor/badge. I was always in Athena/ warrior mode. I was completely unbalanced and I suffered both physically, emotionally and spiritually. I had to be tough. I literally was tough. I was surrounded by men!

Suggested reading: *The Goddess Within* by Jennifer Barker Woolger & Roger Woolger; and *Goddesses in Everywoman* by Jean Shinoda Bolen M.D.

Why activate Athena?

Think of Athena as more of a teacher. She instructed the heroes. She didn't really fight in battle with them. She was intelligent and practical. There are times in our lives where we need to step away from the emotional overload and just focus. Take time to really think things through logically not emotionally. Athena can be a source of strength and wisdom in any situation. She is there to guide and support. She won't do the work for you but she will be there to nudge you along the way.

ACTIVATING AND CONNECTING WITH YOUR INNER WISDOM

Begin by taking a nice deep breath in and slowly let it out. Focused just on your breathing, really feel the changes that take place in your body as you breathe in deeply and exhale fully.

(Pause)

Breathe in … 2 … 3 … 4 … and out … 2 … 3 … 4 …

(Repeat 3 times)

Now breathing at your own pace, breathing fully, breathing easily and staying focused on your breath, I want you to simply use your imagination and picture yourself surrounded by Nature – whatever your safe space in Nature is, see yourself there.

Take a few deep breaths here.

(Pause for breaths)

Now that you are fully relaxed and your mind is calm, I want you to see yourself standing on the edge of a cliff. Knowing that you are perfectly safe, just take note of the scenery. The cliff represents your current life and the scenery in front of you reflects all of the many choices, issues or dilemmas you may be facing. Standing here, your feet bare on the earth (either dirt or rocks), look out and see the world – your world. As you breathe, here on the edge of the cliff, you feel someone approaching.

As this person approaches, you feel very calm. As this person (who you realize to be a woman) stands next to you, she places her hand upon your right shoulder, assuring you that you are not alone and that you are safe.

As you turn to face her, you are surprised to see her wearing an ancient Greek helmet and body armor. She carries in one hand a spear and on her wrist a snake sits coiled, at her feet is a very large shield and sitting on her shoulder is an owl. You ask her why she has decided to meet you at the edge of a cliff.

The Goddess Athena smiles and asks you: "When are you not standing at the edge of a cliff? For life is made up of many decisions that can be both frightening and exciting. There are always going to be opportunities placed before you where you can choose to fall, jump or fly. Let's focus on something big in your life that you are facing – maybe a career decision or something pertaining to your home life – whatever it is, see it in front of you.

Now that you see it, what is in your highest good? How can you utilize wisdom to address this issue?"

(Pause)

Standing at the edge of this cliff, knowing that you are not alone and that you have all the power to overcome obstacles, move mountains and create your existence, let's take some time to just fly.

Athena moves so she is standing behind you. She places both her hands on your shoulders and gives you the power of flight. See your arms turning into large owl wings – feel the feathers.

When you are ready, move to the very edge of the cliff. Looking out at all the obstacles and challenges in your life, see yourself lift off the cliff and take flight. See what it is like to "rise" above these issues.

See your life with a new sense of sight. Utilize owl's sharp keen vision. As you fly, just observe your life with a new perspective. Take a few deep breaths here to just enjoy the power of flight.

When you decide to land, you join Athena and give her thanks for sharing owl wisdom with you.

She embraces you and reminds you that you are more powerful than you can even begin to imagine. Standing on this mountain, at the edge of this cliff, you can feel how powerful you really are.

Before Athena leaves, she gives you one last message: "Remember sister that there are no limits to what a woman can do with her intellect and creative ability."

With that, she places a feather in your hand and leaves.

Holding this feather, take a deep breath and remember what it was like to fly and rise above and see things with a new perspective.

You can do this at any time in your life. When you are having a bad day or an uncomfortable situation presents itself, remember that you can push pause, reevaluate and see things with owl's keen eyesight. Change your perspective and change your initial reaction. Rise above.

See yourself turning away from the cliff and slowly make your way back to the present.

Feel your toes and fingers beginning to move as each breath you take brings you back to the room, feeling calm, wise and confident.

THE MORRIGAN

Her many names: Great Queen, Phantom Queen, Morrigu, Morgane, Morrighan, Morgan Le Fay, Triple Goddess (Ana – maiden, Badh – mother cauldron, Macha – crone), Water Goddess. Bird Goddess who transformed herself into a crow. Earth Goddess. Irish Kali. She is not an evil goddess. She is also birth, the midwife, the healer and sometimes the Moon. Celtic Goddess of War. Queen of Demons. Lady of the Lake and Magick. Patroness of priestesses and witches. Queen of the Fairies. Black Raven.

Morrigan was associated with birth and death: she was the goddess that moved the souls through these cycles. She ruled over rivers and lakes. Morrigan was one of the Tuatha de Danann (the tribe of the Goddess Danu). She is a shapeshifter. Morrigan is also known as the matron of revenge, night, magic and prophecy.

As a shapeshifter, she would often appear in the form of an old crone with a cape of raven feathers. At others times, she would take on the shapes of banshee, crow, falcon, raven or wolf.

Her story: her first appearance in literature is found in the *Book of Isaiah*. In this book she is described as a "monster in female form." In other early texts, she comes from a cult called "The Mothers" – this cult was known for battle and regeneration.

Her Spouse: The Dagda, the prominent god in Celtic mythology and leader of the Tuatha De Danaan Dagda. He is considered the God of Earth and Treaties, Master of Magic – a fearsome warrior and a skilled artisan. He was also considered ruler over life and death. He was the son of the Goddess Danu and the God Elada, and he was the father of the Goddess Brigid and God Aengus. His wife was Morrigan.

Their story: when he first saw her, she was bathing along the river bank. Long pale limbs, her skin the color of polished bone. Clever hands loosed the nine tresses upon her head, leaving her hair to spill down her back. It was the black of a starless night, with the glossy sheen of a raven's feathers. She sang softly as she poured the water over her porcelain skin. The song was both somber and joyful, filled with all the pain and ecstasy that was life. Something roused in him at the sight. He knew this woman. Some called her Death, others knew her as Battle – but all he could see now was a painful, dangerous beauty that he longed to make his own. He didn't realize he had moved towards the bank until she was already in his arms. She looked up at him with dark, raven eyes that mirrored his own passion. He laughed to himself, perhaps it seemed odd that the God of Life and the Goddess of Death should make such a passionate union together. But as the Sun sank and the old year died, he happily died in the ecstasy of her love, knowing with the dawn he would rise again, reborn. The Morrigan may bring death, but Dagda knew her true gift was rebirth.

This story depicts a sacred marriage between the king and goddess of the land. Their union is celebrated on Samhain – the night connected with life and death.

Her strengths: fearsome, strong, powerful and enchanting.

Her weaknesses: she is vindictive, killing a person she loves when he failed to recognize who she was.

Her animals: crows, ravens and wolves.

Her plants: mugwort, yew, willow and Irish moss.

Her colors: red and black.

Her libations: moon blood (blood sacrifice), red wine, ale, apples and whiskey.

Her gemstones: onyx, clear quartz, rubies and obsidian.

Her elements: fire and water.

Festivals: January 7th, Feast of the Morrigan.

Her message: as a protectress, she empowers an individual to confront challenges with great personal strength, even against seemingly overwhelming odds.

How the Morrigan will speak to you: nightmares, hauntings and psychic encounters are her way of gaining your attention. Please don't seek her advice or assistance lightly. She is considered a dark goddess, similar to Lilith. You must be ready to see what she shows you. Remember that she is a shapeshifter and she will help you to shift things in your life. SHE IS NOT A GENTLE GODDESS. She will push until she gets your attention. Morrigan will help you delve into your soul and find your strength. She will help you conquer your will and discover your heroic self. She offers you greatness and will protect you. The Morrigan is primarily associated with battle, conflicts, bloodshed and destruction. She was so powerful that it was believed that she could revive dead soldiers so that they could continue fighting the battle. She was an omen of war much like ravens (who would feed on bodies and gather souls and terrorize armies into dying from fear with their shrieking cries). The Morrigan was a great witch and sorceress. She would use spells and incantations as her main weapon. She would also fight in battle.

INVITING MORRIGAN MEDITATION

Let's begin, as always, with our breath. Taking a nice deep breath in, going through each part of your body and consciously relaxing each muscle as you breathe. When you are ready, close your eyes and allow yourself to sink into a deep state of peace and relaxation. Continue this breathing technique until all the tension is exhaled from your body.

(Pause)

Now that you are relaxed, in your mind's eye see yourself sitting on the grass on top of a small hill, there is a large oak tree giving you shade and support. Towards the bottom of the hill you see a bridge. There is a slight breeze but it is a warm sunny day. The heat on your skin is refreshing. Sitting on the hill, looking down at the bridge, just take a few deep breaths here and wait until the Morrigan appears. She will appear to you when you are ready and in whatever form she chooses. Just breathe and wait.

(Pause)

When the Morrigan appears, either approach her or wait for her to approach you. As Goddess of Destruction, she will either help you destroy and strip clean the issues of chaos or conflict in your life or she will help you fight through them. If you are not wanting to do either, then ask her to simply take away those issues. Give them to her freely.

If you are seeking a clearer path or a new direction, she will give you the vision of raven that you may be able to see things differently, from a higher perspective. Raven is magick.

Be alert and pay attention to the signs, signals and omens you have already been receiving or will receive when raven is invited into your life.

If you are seeking empowerment and strength, the Morrigan may give you the power of wolf. Activating wolf awakens ancient wisdom, deeply rooted in the earth and sacred mysteries.

Spend some time with the Morrigan. Embrace her ancient, unique and mysteriously fierce energy.

(Pause)

When working with the Morrigan, it is important to show her respect by giving her an offering. See yourself placing whatever offering you choose into her hands. Once she has received your offering, see her mysteriously vanish.

Focus on your breath one more time. Breathing in deeply and exhaling fully. As you focus on your breath, feel yourself coming back to the present and back to your body. Feel your feet beginning to move, your hands beginning to move. When you are ready, come back to the room.

FREYA

Freya: her name means "lady". She is the Norse Goddess of Love, Sex, Beauty, Fertility, War and Death. Freya rules over the afterlife. She collects half the souls that die in battle and the other go to Odin's hall in Valhalla. To a Viking, death is an honor. Freya is rumored to have slept with ALL the gods and elves and even her brother. She is a seeker of passion, pleasures and thrills. Ultimately, Freya is the archetype of the Volva – a professional practitioner of Seidr, the most organized form of Norse magic. It was Freya who introduced this art to the gods and to humans. She is master at controlling and manipulating the desires, health and prosperity of others. She was rumored to have "loose" sexual practices.

Freya's tribe: the Vanir, which is a group of gods and goddesses associated with nature, wild places, animals and unseen realms. She is an honorary member of the Aesir gods. Her father is Njord and her mother unknown. Freyr is her brother. Together they represented the untamed forces of Nature. Her husband is Odr, who is also known as Odin. Freya is identical to Frigg. Both Frigg and Freya were accused of infidelity to Odin. Because we know that goddesses are interchangeable, it is possible that Frigg and Freya are one and the same.

Her role as Volva: Freya is Goddess of Magic and Divination. Seidr is a form of shamanic Norse magic. This particular type of magic is focused on creating one's destiny. A Volva is a sorceress, making her highly ambiguous, exalted and feared. For example, in one myth she was said to possess falcon feathers that allow their bearer to shift his or her shape into a falcon. Freya was the one that taught Odin Seidr and in return he gave her his knowledge of runes.

Her necklace: Her beauty was rumored to be so extraordinary that no man could resist her. Especially when she was wearing her necklace called the Brisingamen. This necklace was made for her by four Dwarves. It was rumored that she slept with each Dwarf. Freya was leader of the Valkyries – beautiful maidens of Odin who brought the souls of slain warriors chosen by Odin to Valhalla. It is said she as goddess gets first pick of the slain warriors. In modern times she has become associated with the fairy realm and spirit realm. She is able to travel to all of the nine worlds in Nordic cosmology. It is said that the Northern Lights are caused by Freya traveling through the night sky with the Valkyries.

Her myth and legend: Freya has blonde hair, wears a helmet and carries a sword. She is depicted riding a chariot pulled by two large blue cats given to her by Thor. Other legends say she rides a battle swine. She has a cloak of feathers which enables her to shapeshift into a raven.

Her strengths: female sexuality, wild and untamed, force of nature.

Her sacred animals: cats and wild boars.

Her most sacred animal: the raven.

Her plants: cowslips, daisies and primroses.

Gemstone: amber.

Her attributes: shapeshifter, lover and warrior.

Call upon Freya: when you are in need of your warrior spirit, when you need to stand up for yourself and your rights, when you need to set boundaries, take control of your life and ditch the role of victim.

Her day is Friday! Call upon Freya when you want to own your sexual energy and erotic impulses. She will help you to express your sexual power. Freya will help you to express, both physically and verbally, your needs in the bedroom. She will also help you to be more exact with who and what you are wanting to attract into your life – whether that be a new lover, better lover or a different form of your passion. Fire energy doesn't always have to evolve around sex; it can be career, family or something else. See your sexual energy as an on and off switch that you are in control of.

Frigg was Odin's official wife, but it has been determined that she is an exact duplication of Freya, making them one and the same. When referenced to his connection with Freya, Odin was called Od. When referenced with his connection to Frigg, Odin was called Odin. Whether you choose to see them as two different deities with incredible similarities or as one main deity, that is really up to you. For me, I embrace them as two halves of a whole. For, to me, all Women are split in a way. There is a side of all women that is soft, loving, nurturing and devoted – this is what I classify as the Frigg or all-mother side. Then there is a side of all women that is passionate, mysterious and confident in her sexuality – this is what I classify as the Freya side. Both Freya and Frigg hold in their possessions falcon feathers or wings of the falcon.

Creating an altar to Freya: as Goddess of Love, Sexuality and Confidence; red and gold are her power colors. She is a queen after all. Often Freya is called upon to activate self-love, passion for one's own body and sexual freedom. A nice long bath with scented oils, bath bombs or fresh rose petals is a way to activate and invite Freya energy. The power really comes into giving yourself permission to be a sexual queen. There is a reason everyone wanted to sleep with Freya. Who doesn't want a taste of someone that confident, that sure of one's self. Freya didn't need to sleep with anyone to obtain any special powers, she liked sex and she used it to her advantage. She wanted the Brisingamen necklace, which is a torc (a symbol of one's power). She slept with the Dwarves in exchange for the necklace but she did that because she wanted to. She may not have been attracted to the Dwarves but she wanted that necklace and she got it.

Journal prompt: When we call upon any deity, we are daring to see ourselves as we see them. We are asking them to be a mirror to us and show us what we are capable of. So, with Freya, what attribute of hers are you wanting to see within yourself?

Her rune is Fehu: the rune of fulfillment and abundance, of breaking through your own barriers and giving thanks, for there is much to be thankful for. This rune is a reminder of the barriers you create and you must break. Having an attitude of gratitude can take you far.

MEDITATION ACTIVATION WITH FRIGG/ FREYA

Move into a meditative state by focusing on your breath. Inhaling to the count of four and exhaling to the count of four. Keep this breath pattern going until you are able to visualize that you are sitting beside a large fire in the center of a long house. The fire is warm and beside you sits a woman that you know must be Frigg.

See that Frigg stands up and moves away from the fire leaving the long house. Staring into the flames you watch as each flame dances its own dance, spiraling upwards, sparking and popping. You hear a door close behind you and as you turn to look to see who has entered the room, you see a tall elegant woman.

She is dressed in deep colors of red; her hair has hints of gold and copper. She looks as if she is made of fire. She moves gracefully, with poise and confidence. She doesn't join you beside the fire, instead she sits at a table holding a large gold bowl. She places the bowl upon the table and begins to pour water into it. She doesn't seem to care that you are watching. In fact, she knows you are watching and she seems to be putting on a show for you. She pours the water with such ease and pleasure. You see her lips curl back, showing the most stunning smile, even her eyes sparkle.

You can't help but get up and move towards her. There seems to be a magnetic pull. You place your mead horn on your chair and you get up and move cautiously towards the beautiful woman who is staring into the water-filled bowl. Her eyes gaze up at you as you approach and your heart seems to skip a beat, caught in your chest for just a moment by her captivating beauty. Around her neck is the most stunning necklace of gold with one very large amber stone that hangs between her large, voluptuous breasts. She stands and offers you her chair, gently caressing your arm from your shoulder down as you sit, her fingers soft like rose petals.

You tingle all over from just this simple touch. She offers a light chuckle. As you sit she moves to stand behind you and slowly she begins to run her fingers through your hair. Pulling it back, she asks you to look into the water.

As you look down into the water, expecting to see your reflection, you see so much more! You see your face but it is soft, clean and sparkling. You see your hair flowing, shiny, with tiny intricate braids and flowers woven into each strand. You see your lips full and alive, hungry! You see your eyes as you have never seen them before. You ask out loud: "Is this really me?"

The beautiful woman sits down across from you and reaches out her hands to hold yours. You know this woman to be Freya, for her beauty is a legend that all know. She caresses your hands with her soft delicate fingers and gives you a gentle squeeze. Her reply is simple:

"When you love yourself fully, you see yourself fully. So, love, that is the key. Just love."

(Pause)

Follow with invocation:

"Freya, she whose name means lady. Goddess of Love, War, Sex, Life and Death. Sun Goddess.
Lady of Fire. She who moves and dances like flames. Sorceress. She who teaches magick.
Goddess Freya we call to you. Goddess Freya we welcome you."

So, your journey this evening has come to an end but your journey to connect and activate self-love has just begun. Take some time this week and give yourself one night. Draw a healing bath, sit in a pool under the moonlight, take an intentional healing shower, light some candles and incense and spend some time honoring you, for you too are goddess.

Journal your meditation experience.

NYX

"Goddess of the Night"

Nyx: a Greek goddess.

Her many names: Nox, Night, Primordial Goddess, Mother of Demons, Dark Mother, personification of night, mother of many deities.

How she is depicted: as a winged goddess, sometimes riding a chariot, clothed in dark and accompanied by stars as her consorts.

Her stones: agate (keeps bad dreams away) and moonstone (to honor her). Moonstone is a reflection of the person who wears it.

Her scents: myrtle, camphor, aloe, white rose and white poppy.

Libations: grapes, dark red wine, eggs and dragon fruit.

Colors: black, silver, grey or white.

Animals: bats and owls.

Time of year: Yule.

Her legend: Nyx emerged as the dawn of creation. Born a child of Chaos and Air, she coupled with Erebos (darkness) and produced Aither (light) and Hemera (day).

She is one of the ancient protogenoi or primordial gods – the basic components of the Universe, the firstborn elemental goddess. She was not born on this Earth. She was born before Gaia was created. In fact, Gaia is her sister. She alone birthed a hoard of dark spirits including the Three Fates: sleep, death and strife She is a very ancient deity. She is known as the subduer of gods and men; even Zeus himself stood in awe of her and even feared her. She was the only goddess that was more powerful and older than Zeus. While she is mentioned very little in Greek mythology, she was said to be a figure of exceptional power and beauty. She is literally in the shadows, as the shadows. She was a shadowy figure that comes in glimpses.

Her power: Nyx can be both a help to mankind and a hindrance. She can bring you either sleep or death, depending on the situation. She embodies sacred mystery, divine wisdom and dark artistry. She is short-tempered and jealous. Nyx is the shadow made divine, for if we only have the courage to understand and embrace the darkness, we find that all things are possible and nothing is out of reach if we only give it form. Nyx has no limits.

"She walks in beauty
like the night
upon darkened hills
under starlit skies
bless the Moon
full tonight
and enchanted magic
elemental light
in the name of the
goddess
the daughter
and the elements."

Danielle – *templeofnyx.blogspot.com*

When to call upon Nyx: when you need to reach your original true essence and awareness. Call to her when the night is dark – during a New Moon or Dark Moon. Call to her anytime you are in need of cleansing, protection, awareness of self and fertility.

Spell to Nyx: at sunset, carve your wish on a black candle. Concentrate on your desire, see it clearly in your mind, see the image filling the candle and invoke Nyx. Black-winged night, Dark Mother Nyx, all things are born from your darkness. From the dark of our mothers' wombs we are born, from the dark soil the seed germinates and grows. From the dark of the underworld our spirits are reborn. Nyx, as you wrap your dark cloak over the world, I recognize that night is a time of beginnings. In the dark womb of night let my spell form and grow. Mother Night, hear my prayer.

Mentions of Nyx: in the TV vampire series, *House of Night*, Nyx plays the key role of Goddess of Vampires. This series has launched Nyx into the forefront of popular culture. More and more teen groups are dedicating themselves to the service of Nyx. In 2005, a moon near Pluto was discovered and named in her honor. Also, there is a cosmetic brand called Nyx. She is also a fictional character in the Marvel Comics universe. There is also a video game in her honor called *"Smite"*.

The God Chaos: the origin of everything and the first thing that ever existed. The primordial void. The first primordial deities emerged out of Chaos.

Powers of chaos: by definition, chaos is a state of utter confusion, disorder, total lack of organization or order.

- Have any of you been experiencing some form of chaos in your lives?
- What are you willing to birth in this state of chaos?

Nyx: reminds us that it is easy to get caught up in the delusions around our suffering, our misfortunes, our fears – our chaos. She encourages us to lift the veils of illusion and awaken our power and dismantle blame so that wholeness can be found within. She is here to remind us that we have more potential than we realize, if we would only open ourselves and our hearts to her.

Nox: this is her Roman name. Known as Night, the oldest of the deities. She was held in great esteem among the ancients. Some believe her to be even older than Chaos. All things had their beginning from her. She is primal in a way that even the mightiest of gods must fear. Nox is mother to them all. Barely seen but found in darkness, clothed in black, she glides between the light, just at the edge of vision.

A spectre. She loves and protects all her children equally. They are her calling and her curse, her greatest pride and deepest shame.

Powers of the New Moon: the New Moon is a time to plant seeds for the future. Quite a bit of internal work takes place when the Moon is dark. This is an excellent time to focus on healing. Look within to discover what you really want and what you no longer need. The New Moon is a time to focus on your desires, dreams and what you are wanting to manifest and help grow.

- What are you manifesting?
- What are you willing to do to help that grow?
- What dream is hidden deep within in the dark?

MEDITATION TO CONNECT WITH NYX

Let's start by getting into a comfortable position, closing our eyes and just focusing on our breath.

Let's take a deep breath in and exhale it out. Breathe in and out.

(Repeat 3 times)

Now breath in … 2 … 3 … 4 … and out … 2 … 3 … 4.

(Repeat 3 times)

Now breathing at your own pace, breathing fully and breathing easily, give your body permission to relax and let go. Exhale any stresses or tensions in your face, your neck, your shoulders, your arms, your chest, your torso, your hips, your legs and your feet. Just breathe.

Now that you are relaxed, I want you to simply use your imagination and picture yourself standing outside in a safe space in Nature. It is very very dark and there is no light at all. In fact, it is hard to even see your own outstretched hand. You know you are safe, but there is still the slightest bit of fear in the darkness. You are warm and the air is thick and feels reminiscent of a hug, the kind you never want to end. You keep waiting for your eyes to adjust but it stays quite dark. This darkness is known as Chaos. This is what we felt in the womb of our mothers. In the great caves where women sat in ancient circles. Even in the darkness we as women can find security and comfort.

Take a few deep breaths here in the dark of night, the shadows.

As you stand here, just breathing, you begin to feel quite restless, possibly frustrated, maybe even angry. You long for some source of light. Something, anything! Just when you are about to panic, a faint light appears above you. A tiny star. Soon the entire sky is filled with stars and you begin to feel peace and some shred of hope. There is no Moon to light the way, only stars. You have heard that out of the underworld our spirits are reborn, that seeds germinate best in dark places and night is the time of beginnings. Are you ready to embrace the power of the shadows and begin to grow?

While you stand here, you see a tall shadow approaching, you can just barely make out that this is a figure coming towards you. The closer this person gets, the more you can see that they are clothed in a very dark cloak. You may step back at first but the person just continues to walk towards you.

Soon this person is right in front of you. Take a deep breath and know that you are safe.

Watch as this person removes their cloak.

Standing in front of you is a very tall, elegant woman, with very pale almost iridescent skin. She is completely clothed in black, even her hair is black, but her skin is so white it literally brightens the night sky and you can begin to make out your surroundings, just by the light radiating off her skin. This is the Goddess Nyx – she who was born from Chaos and lives in the shadows. She has appeared before you to give you light, to help you see your way in the darkness. Standing in front of you, she reaches her hand out and places her palm flat on your chest, resting over your heart. She softly gazes into your eyes and asks you: "What is it you are most afraid of here in the dark?"

(Pause)

What shadows have you been hiding from?

(Pause)

She listens, intently – for once, someone has really heard you. She offers no solution, she just listens. When she removes her hand there is a shining light on your chest. She has placed a star on your chest.

She tells you that the answers and light you are seeking in the dark places of your soul have always been with you: "For you are the light in the darkness. Only you can fix your life, mend the hurts, heal yourself and activate the traits that you long to embrace. No one is going to take that responsibility but you. No one is responsible for you but you. No one is going to create change for you but you. Chaos in life is growth, embrace it or hide from it in the shadows, but only you can give yourself permission to grow. Without darkness, there would be no light. So it is ok to go into the darker places of your mind, it's ok to have bad days, hurt feelings and anger. These are things we are taught to fear and not allow, but these are chaos and we have to embrace these moments to truly step into our most authentic selves. Learn to allow, honor and respect all of your emotions without blame. Only love. For these are feelings that you embrace, no one gives them to you. No one can *make* you feel anything. You have the absolute power. So, learn to breathe. Learn to love and accept yourself."

The Goddess Nyx places a small token in your hand and gives you a kiss on the forehead. As you stand here with your heart glowing in starlight, you ponder her words. How many times have you blamed someone else for your chaos, for your feelings? How many times have you become upset with yourself for being angry, hurt or frustrated? These are moments of growth. Give yourself gratitude that you can feel so deeply. By accepting that these are feelings that we have chosen, we actually lessen the duration of them. We learn to love and accept ourselves for ourselves. It is normal to have what some would call "bad" moments, but isn't it truly beautiful to feel so deeply and passionately?

Give yourself love. Life in chaos is beautiful and will make you stronger.

When you are ready, take a nice deep breath in and exhale it out.

Now breathe in love for you, all of you, and exhale any doubts, fears, inhibitions or insecurities.

Just breathe.

Nyx teaches us to be the light for ourselves – to pick ourselves up, for we are the ones that create our lives. We are not puppets on a string. We are not victims. Take another deep breath in and exhale it out. With each breath, allow yourself to slowly and gently come back to the present, feeling forgiveness, love and acceptance – for you are beautiful inside and out.

When you are ready, open your eyes and come back to the room.

MEDUSA

"Guardian or Protectress"

Her origins: some know her to be a Greek goddess, but others know her to be an African Snake Goddess.

Her family: Medusa was the daughter of Phorcys (God of the Sea) and Ceto, a female Sea Goddess. She was sister to Sthenno and Euryale, but Medusa was the only mortal out of three sisters.

Appearance: some say that she was hideously ugly with the body of a dragon and her hair was made up of poisonous snakes. Other myths say that she was a beautiful woman who was a priestess for the Goddess Athena.

One story: as a priestess for Athena, Medusa was a golden-haired maiden, fully devoted to Athena. She, as a priestess, practiced celibacy. However, Poseidon wooed her and she fell in love with him and forgot her vows. She and Poseidon were caught in the throes of passion inside Athena's temple by Athena herself. Athena was outraged and decided to punish Medusa by turning each golden strand of her hair into a poisonous snake; her eyes she turned into bloodshot, furious orbs and her milky white skin into a disgusting green. Medusa was disgusted by her appearance and fled her home. She was shunned by the world. In her despair, she fled to Africa where it is said that young snakes would fall from her head and that is how, according to the Greeks, Africa became a home to venomous reptiles. With the curse of Athena upon her, she turned everyone who gazed upon her into stone.

Another version: Poseidon was so captivated by Medusa's beauty that he snuck into Athena's temple and raped Medusa. When Medusa ran to Athena to get help after the raping, Athena was so disgusted and outraged that she cursed Medusa, for Athena was a servant to the male hierarchy.

Medusa and Perseus: Medusa, being a great guardian, led an army to battle against Perseus, who later killed Medusa in her sleep – a subtle act of male control.

Another story: in Africa, Medusa was one third of the Triple Moon Goddess. In pre-dynastic Egypt, she was known as Neith, and in Libya (her homeland) the Triple Moon Goddess was called Anatha. Ancient inscriptions about the North African Goddess give this description:

> "I have come from myself. I am all that has been and that will be, and no mortal has yet been able to lift the veil that covers me."

Sovereign female wisdom: as the African Goddess, Medusa was very beautiful. The snakes that the Greeks refer to as being her hair were really dreadlocks – which are a sacred connection to the divine. Some have even linked Medusa to "Mami Wata" (a West African Vodoun) or the Divine African Mother, Prophetess, Holy Widow, Self-creator, the one who reigned alone in the beginning, the one who brings forth the gods, she who was mateless and the Virgin Mother.

Medusa the matriarchal goddess: her hair was snakes and her body that of the dragon and this would represent transformation, shedding the skin and begin reborn. Both the snake and the dragon are symbols of the divine feminine. As women, we are reborn every 28 days. It would make sense that Medusa was a Goddess of Menstruation. A woman's cycle synchronizes with the cycles of the Moon and the ocean. Medusa is literally portrayed as the embodiment of all things feminine. She was depicted as having wings which symbolize the sky, freedom and mastery over worlds. Some say she even had boar tusks protruding from her mouth – the pig in Greek mythology was a symbol of birth and fertility. Medusa was very powerful; she controlled the natural cycle and lived in harmony with the worlds of earth and sky. However, she was a great threat to the Greek male gods and because of this she was beheaded. Her head is used to further encourage the dominion of the male over the destructive, sexual, empowered female.

The Wise one,
The Keeper of the Dark Moon Mysteries,
Goddess of Death and Rebirth.

- As an AMAZON priestess, she wore a leather pouch around her waist that contained live snakes, representing wisdom and renewal. She carried the Gorgon mask, its purpose was to frighten off the uninitiated and help to protect the secrecy surrounding the magic of the Dark Moon. The mask was painted red to symbolize the power of menstrual blood.
- Goddess of Divination, Healing, Magic and Sexual Kundalini Serpent Mysteries. To invoke her wisdom, the priestesses would wear Medusa masks and celebrate the sexual rites with the Sea Gods.

Athena and Medusa, one in the same: in Jungian terms, Medusa is Athena's shadow. Athena was a chaste virgin who lived to serve her father, Zeus, with Medusa as her shadow-self – dark and sexual. Athena, in essence, attacked and cursed her very shadow-self. Medusa, Goddess of Wisdom, Death and Renewal, Dark Goddess of Healing and Divination, she who represented the goddess-worshipping Libyan AMAZON priestesses is ultimately destroyed by the patriarchal invading Greeks. Her truth was twisted and she was first turned from a gentle, loving Dark Mother into a monster by her own maiden/Athena-self.

Athena's punishment: at first the great beloved maiden aspect of the Libyan Moon Goddess, she was then ripped from her AMAZON sisters and turned into a traitor. She was forced into obedience to her father – the God Zeus. She was not even given a mother. She was Warrior Goddess who fought against her own goddess-worshipping sisters. She was made to kill her own dark, wise and sexual self (Medusa) and wore the image of this slaughter on her breastplate as a reminder of what she and all women under patriarchy have lost.

Working with your shadow: the shadow is an archetype that forms part of the unconscious mind and is composed of repressed ideas, instincts, impulses, weaknesses, desires, perversions and embarrassing fears. This is our wildness, our chaos and our unknown.

- Accept it – accepting your darkness will allow you to take responsibility for yourself, and once you truly acknowledge your dark traits instead of avoiding them, they will stop having control over you.
- Experience your shadow-self – journey into the dark, visit the unknown parts of you that have been hidden away. Reconcile and unify.
- Own it – those traits that you are ashamed of or embarrassed by, the traits that others have rejected – embrace them, own them. By owning them, you actually open the door to happiness, fulfillment and true enlightenment.

What are some of your shadow traits?

Mirror work has always been very powerful for me. I was taught that anger was unbecoming of a lady. Over the years, I embraced my rage – not always in healthy ways, but I let it surface. Now, when I get angry or rage, I do so in a productive way – focusing my anger on housework or maybe a project I have been putting off, or by simply sitting in contemplation and asking myself: what am I really angry about?

GODDESS MEDUSA ACTIVATION

Let's begin by getting into a comfortable position. Allow your eyes to gently close and just focus on your breath. Take a nice deep inhale and exhale it fully. Allow your body to relax, releasing all tension with each exhale that you take.

Breathe in … 2 … 3 … 4 … and out … 2 … 3 … 4.

(Repeat)

Now that your body is relaxed, I want you to see yourself in a safe space. This can be a place in Nature, your favorite room in your home or a new place. Feel your body relax here as you take in your surroundings. Allow yourself to feel calm, anchored and at peace. This is where your conscious mind will rest while we journey into your subconscious. Tapping into your mind's eye and using your imagination, I want you to activate your subconscious mind and allow yourself to feel your feet standing on a cold stone floor. You are now within a Greek temple. There are large pillars of stone and you can see Nature all around. Standing in this temple, you become aware that you are not alone.

You may feel a presence moving quietly, circling you. To your right there is a very large mirror.

You approach the mirror and are confused at the reflection you see. It is you but it is your shadow-self. Before you stands the you that you keep hidden. This reflection may be sad, angry or sexual, but this is you – the part of you that society has taught you to repress and not allow to surface.

Take a deep breath here and allow yourself to see your shadow.

(Pause)

You hear the presence moving closer and you see her reflection in the mirror – a beautiful woman, her breasts exposed, her body moving in a slithering motion as if she is not all human.

Her hair flows and moves as if it is alive itself. As she slithers up behind you, her shape becomes clearer. Her hair is alive with hundreds of snakes; her body itself appears to be some kind of reptile. She is covered with scales from the waist down.

She is stunning and captivating but something inside you is warning you to not turn around and look directly at her. Something in her eyes gives you a warning. She is Medusa the Great Goddess.

Together you both stand, gazing into the mirror.

(Pause)

As she moves in closer, you can feel her breath on your neck and you see and feel her hand position itself on your shoulder. You shudder at her cold touch but part of you feels very calm and safe.

She encourages you to continue to look into the mirror and, as you do, your reflection begins to shift and move, almost as if you are watching yourself on a television screen. Your reflection is acting out all those shadow traits that you have been fighting too long to acknowledge. Medusa is here to give you strength as you acknowledge and own your shadow-self. She has the gentle touch of a mother.

You are not afraid of her but incredibly overcome with gratitude. You decide to turn around and face her. She slowly backs up and at first appears to be frightened by your willingness to see her without the aid of a mirror, for she has been made a monster for many centuries, but still you turn and you look at her as if you would a dear friend. Nothing happens. You don't turn to stone like the stories foretold.

You in return are seen as well.

(Pause)

How beautiful to be seen as you really are. No costumes, no layers to hide under. Just seen.

Medusa holds out her arms to you and you embrace each other as old friends, for you and Medusa are the same. You hug each other so tightly that you become one. You, like Medusa, have had stories told about you, very hurtful ones. You have at one point or another been painted out to be a monster for the mere fact that you are female. You came to this temple today to heal that old hurt, whether from this lifetime or lifetimes passed. You carry within you her strength, passion and independence. See yourself moving in a very graceful almost slithering motion as you leave the temple and slowly return back to your safe space. Focusing on your breathing once more, taking a nice deep inhale, feeling your body once again anchor and ground itself back into your conscious state - breathe in and breathe out.

Allow each breath to carry you back to the room, back to the present.

KALI

"Goddess of Enlightenment or Liberation"

Kali: a Hindu goddess.

Her many names: Kali Ma, Black Mother, Great Mother Goddess, Shakit, The Feminine Force, Universal Mother, Dark Mother.

Strengths: fierce, potent, healer, loving, destroyer, wild, protector, compassionate, liberator.

Her colors: red and black – "in black, all colors merge."

Her stones: obsidian, black tourmaline and fire agate.

Her scents: jasmine, rose and sandalwood.

Her libations: wine.

Kali is depicted as having black or blue skin to represent the darkness that she removes from humans. She wears a garland of 50 men's skulls as a necklace. This is the number of letters in the Sanskrit alphabet and symbolizes knowledge and wisdom. She wears a skirt of dismembered arms because the ego arises out of identification with the body. She pokes her tongue out of her mouth and has four arms. In one hand she holds a severed head dripping blood and in the other three sacred weapons. One hand removes fears and the others grant bliss. She is naked, free from all covering and illusions. She is a full-breasted mother, for she creates endlessly. She is a symbol of domination over the world, or the world of men where ego has become the center of life. She is the bright fire of truth, not hidden by the trappings of ignorance. She brings death to the ego, which makes her a Goddess of Death. Kali believes that it is our attachment to our physical body that gives rise to the ego within. Kali will grant liberation by removing the illusion of the ego. Kali is the most compassionate goddess because she provides "moksha", or liberation, to her children. She is the counterpart of Lord Shiva the Destroyer.

Her story: Kali is one of India's most popular goddesses. Her picture hangs in many homes. Calcutta is her temple city and derives its name from the phrase Kali-Ghatt or "steps of Kali." The original temple was a very small hut. The current temple was completed in 1809. Mention of Kali first appeared in the Devi Mahatmya Text (Glory of the Goddess) in the fifth century. She is depicted as not only the Source of Life; she is the very earth, all-creating and all-consuming.

Diwali or the Hindu New Year celebrated on October 30th: women decorate their homes with rice paintings and sand mandalas. More than one billion Hindus all over the world celebrate this festival. There is usually a big feast and merriment. For good luck, they worship Kali who is the Universal Mother Goddess. Diwali is the celebration of victory of good over evil. In the early morning, everyone greets their friends and families, forgiving wrongdoings from the past. They take an oil bath and pray to Kali to destroy their ignorance. They light fireworks to chase away the evil spirits. Diwali is known as a harvest celebration.

Kali's festival: is Mother's Day in India, celebrated on May 8th. Indian women are given new clothes and jewelry and are held in high regard with great reverence.

Kali teaches that pain, sorrow, decay, destruction and death cannot be overcome by denying them or explaining them. They are inevitable. Kali teaches us that we need to accept these things as part of our existence. Kali is Mother. She reveals our mortality to us and releases us to act fully and freely. Kali will aid you in putting an end to issues, relationships, partnerships and things that bring you unhappiness. Kali is the vibrating, motivating energy of the Universe. She literally holds a sword to cut all that separates us from our true nature. Kali comes from the Sanskrit word Kal which means "time". There is nothing that escapes the all-consuming march of time. Kali will swallow your sins and cut off the handcuffs that keep you shackled and tied down. She will take you into the darkness where you will have to face your shadows, demons, skeletons and ghosts. You will need to see them, face them and own them in order to be free from them. Kali Mahadevi is a goddess of creation, preservation and radical transformation. She is the raw female instinct, always changing, always changeless. Without transformation, there is only stagnation. Kali speaks her mind. She lives her passions. She cuts away illusions and distractions to activate change.

- What are your shadows?
- What is it that ego doesn't want you to see?
- What layers are you hiding underneath?

Kali will enter the darkness for you, as you. She will literally "eat" away the darkness that is eating you.

Ego: defined as: "a person's sense of self-esteem or self importance." The ego sees Mother Kali and trembles with fear because the ego sees in her its own demise. A person who is attached to their ego will not be receptive to Mother Kali – they will be scared of her. However, a mature person who engages in spiritual practice to remove the illusion of ego will see Mother

Kali as very sweet, loving, affectionate and overflowing with the most incomprehensible love for her children. For, in truth, we are beings of spirit not flesh. We are not our bodies.

When to call upon Kali: anytime you are feeling overwhelmed, beaten down by anxiety or emotionally paralyzed, to help move forward and escape the demons from your past or present. Surrender to Kali – give the shadows to her, give her your fears, worries and stresses.

BREATHWORK TO RELEASE AND LET KAIL HEAL

Begin by closing your eyes and taking a nice deep breath. Breathe in and breathe out.

(Repeat at least 4 times)

Now take a nice deep breath in and focus on something that is holding you down and, on your exhale, blow it out and catch it in your hands.

Hold it, thank it and toss it to Kali.

Now take a nice deep breath and focus on something that has been stopping you in your tracks, preventing you from moving forward. On your next exhale, blow it out and catch it in your hands.

Hold it, thank it and toss is to Kali.

Keep repeating this until you have released and cleared out any and all tiny little frustrations, self-doubts and insecurities.

Blow it out as you exhale and catch it in your hands.

Hold it, thank it and toss is to Kali.

(Allow some time to pass while clearing is taking place)

Kali will take these worries from you and transform them.
In return you will not be held down by those concerns any longer.
She will free you. Trust her. She is the Mother Kali.

Her chant: "Om Kali Ma" – this mantra vibrates with her power and transports you to her domain. With every inhale, say to yourself silently or out loud: "Om Kali Ma." Feel her infuse your body with her power, radiance and love. With each exhale, breathe out: "Om Kali Ma" and feel her presence fill the Universe around you. Breathe in "Om Kali Ma" and out "Om Kali Ma."

Anyone can work with the Goddess Kali. She is one to be respected and honored like any mother figure, from Mother Mary to Danu the ancient primordial mother. Approach Kali with love and respect. Light a candle and hold her image in your mind or obtain a painting of her.

Call her with a simple chant: close your eyes and recite "Om Kali Ma" until you feel the shift of her energy in the room. Then talk to her just as you would your own mother. Give her your shadows.

MEDITATION TO CONNECT WITH THE GODDESS KALI

Begin by taking a nice deep breath in and exhale it out. When you are ready, close your eyes and just focus on your breath. Breathing in deeply: "Om Kali Ma" and exhaling fully: "Om Kali Ma."

(Repeat this for 4 breaths)

Now that you are relaxed, focus on the energy in the room. Can you feel a presence? Just by breathing and repeating this chant, you have made sacred contact with the Goddess Kali – the Universal Mother.

Stay focused on your breath, repeating silently to yourself on the inhale: "Om Kali Ma" and on the exhale: "Om Kali Ma." Remain with this breath until you see the Goddess Kali in front of you.

Now simply ask her to help you clear out anything that is standing in your way.

Focus on what that may be and ask her to destroy it or transform it.

(Pause for about 5 deep breaths)

The connection you make with the Goddess Kali will be unique and authentic, just like you.

So, allow her to enter this space, knowing that you are safe and that she is a mother archetype.

Allow her to heal you. She loves you. You are one of her children.

Give her this opportunity to take away your pains, aches and sorrows.

Allow her to cut away the illusions and the distractions that are preventing you from moving forward.

(Pause for 4 breaths)

GRATITUDE

To those who made this journey with me, I offer you my heartfelt gratitude.

Writing a book is no small task. Sharing one's devotion to a specific deity is a very vulnerable experience and one that I am sure will meet some criticism.

My life has and will remain a journey of growth and expansion.

Each god, goddess or animal that enters as teacher is one I thank profusely.

As a constant student, I honor each lesson that comes along the way.

Thank you for allowing me to share with you my passion for wolves and Skadi as they have been some of the most life-changing and challenging gods in my life.

– Sincerely yours, Lady Wolf.

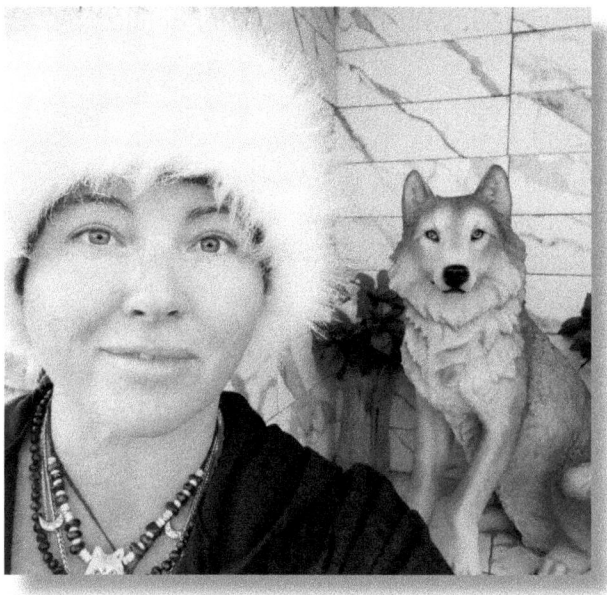

Lady Wolf resides in Southern Utah where, together with her husband of 22 years, she offers service to her community from the Desert Healing Sanctuary (formerly known as the Utah Goddess Temple).

She is a mother of three and "Gigi" to her granddaughter. Lady Wolf began her journey into witchcraft at the age of sixteen. She is an initiated witch and triple-ordained Wiccan high priestess.

She is a reiki master, crystal therapist, green witch, hypnotherapist, chakra healer, initiated Bard and yoga instructor and is currently working her way through the Seidr journey.

As a constant student, Lady Wolf devotes time each day to her studies of the Craft, honoring all the plants and animals as her teachers.

She shares her home with two dogs, three turtles, five birds and seven chickens.

As an animist and shapeshifting priestess, Lady Wolf's passion is in helping individuals, couples and groups connect with their spirit animals.

To connect with Lady Wolf or book her for public speaking events:

- www.utahgoddesstemple.org
- desertsagewitchcraft@gmail.com
- youtube channel: "Lady Wolf"
- facebook: @deserthealingsanctuary or @ladywolfauthor
- Instagram: @ladywolfauthor
- tiktok: ladywolf505

ONLINE RESOURCES FOR SKADI GODDESS OF WINTER & MOTHER OF WOLVES

https://crescentmoonsnowshoes.com/blog/is-snowshoeing-really-harder-than-hiking/
https://hrafnar.org/articles/dpaxson/asynjur/skadi/
https://mythus.fandom.com/wiki/Skadi
https://motherhoodinpointoffact.com/wolf-animal-mothers/
http://www.wolfcountry.net/stories/
http://www.antiquitynow.org-theancientrootsofdisneysblockbusterfilmfrozen
https://theblissfulmind.com/art-of-doing-nothing/
https://fireiceandsteel.wordpress.com/2014/11/04/skadi-and-the-saami-part-1/
https://scandinaviafacts.com/this-is-how-the-vikings-proposed-and-got-married/
http://viking.archeurope.info/index.php?page=viking-marriage-and-divorce
https://www.theatlantic.com/magazine/archive/1966/11/marriage-as-a-wretched-institution/306668/
https://umatter.princeton.edu/respect/relationships/autonomy
http://www.northernpaganism.org/shrines/skadi/gifts.html

BOOKS

Northern Mysteries and Magick by Freya Aswynn.
Baldr's Magic by Nicholas E. Brink.
In Praise of Wolves by R.D. Lawrence.
Ravensong by Catherine Feher Elston.
Wolfsong by Catherine Feher Elston.
Seidr the Gate is Open by Katie Gerrard.
Essential Asatru by Diana Paxson.
Taking up the Runes by Diana Paxson.
The Wisdom of Wolves by Elli H. Radinger.
The Wisdom of Wolves by Jim & Jamie Dutcher.
Among Wolves by Gordon Haber & Marybeth Holleman.
Wolves by Shaun Ellis.
Of Wolves and Men by Barry Holstun Lopez.
Valkyrie by Johanna Katrin Fridriksdottir.
Children of Ash and Elm by Neil Price.

Ingram Content Group UK Ltd.
Milton Keynes UK
UKHW021837280423
420952UK00010B/169

9 781915 580023